A Bathtub in Our Garden

Robert W. Martin

First paperback edition printed 2014 in the United Kingdom
This edition ©2025
ISBN 978-0-992897-40-6
© Robert W. Martin.
A catalogue record for this book is available from the British Library.

Published by Linear Road Press
Suite 10544
PO Box 6945
London W1A 6US

For more copies of this book, please email
info@la-darnoire.com
Although every precaution has been taken in the preparation of this book, the publisher and author assume no responsibility for errors or omissions. Neither is any liability assumed for damages resulting from the use of any information contained herein.

To my wife,
without whom this would never have been written.

Preface

CENTRAL France has a region known as Sologne. It's so central, in fact, that the region is officially given the designation "Centre". This is an area characterised by forest and lakes, and was originally the hunting grounds of the French Kings, until they met an unfortunate end.

In the middle of a triangle of three large towns, Orleans, Blois, and Bourges, lies a long-abandoned farmhouse called La Darnoire. In the local patois, this means "The black earth" (*La Terre Noir*) - probably because the sandy soil is indeed a very dark colour. This neglected farmhouse is being dragged kicking and screaming from the nineteenth century (when it was built) into the twenty-first century. But we are not part of some television programme called "Find Me a Place in the Country" where prospective buyers are assisted by teams of builders, have interior designers and architects on call, have an initial budget of £750 000 and by the end of the programme have spent over £1 million to renovate their dream home.

On the contrary, we have one percent of that type of budget. So any renovations or improvements that are done not only need to be as ecologically-sound as possible, but done as cheaply as possible! And if that means employing some lateral thinking to re-use an object for something else entirely, so much the better!

Cast

(In order of appearance)

LSS .... Long-Suffering-Spouse

FIL .... Father-in-Law

MIL .... The late Mother-in-Law

Aged Aunt .... FIL's sister

(These siblings have not spoken in years)

JP .... Cousin of LSS and favourite nephew of FIL

J .... Female owner of the farm next to that of FIL

Friend F .... Retired friend of LSS

Friend L .... Non-retired friend of LSS

(particularly good at DIY)

M & O .... Retired couple who are in charge of

the local hunt; overall Good Eggs

T & M .... Our closest full-time neighbours.

It just so happens that their house is in the next county.

Introduction

O R, how someone who doesn't speak French ended up in the middle of France...

I'm an African. I was born in Uganda, and because my father didn't like settling down for too long in one place, I also ended up living in Kenya, Tanzania, and Australia. This was before I even started school! By the time I was enrolled in full-time education at the age of six, we were in Namibia (or South West Africa as it was then known). This is probably where I picked up a liking for solitude; Namibia has the second lowest population density per square kilometre than any other country. (Mongolia is the lowest, in case you were wondering). And it's also probably where I picked up the very African ability of lateral thinking and practicality.

By the time I had finished my schooling, I was fluent in Afrikaans, had a smattering of German; and (courtesy of my parents) knew a few words of Swahili. French simply didn't feature. I then moved to South Africa, where in 1987 I obtained a Bachelor of Science degree majoring in Forestry & Nature Conservation from the University of Stellenbosch. Once I had graduated, I was called up for National Service. (This has been discontinued now, of course). Two years later, having reached the dizzying rank of lieutenant in the Infantry Corps, I started working for the Forestry Department. It soon became evident that the majority of my time would be spent behind a desk. Not only that, but the astoundingly low salary meant that I was having to live on my credit card each month. As soon as my salary was paid into my bank account, that brought the credit card balance back to zero. Rinse and repeat.

So after a year I resigned, and joined my brother in a small business selling, hiring, and repairing power tools, and supplying the building trade with necessities. Unfortunately they say you should never work with family, and this proved to be the case, so I left South Africa behind and ventured off to the sunny shores of the United Kingdom where I yet again changed careers. I worked in IT for several years, and also met my wife. She's French, by the way, but by the time we left the UK, she had actually lived there a year longer than I had!

When the recession hit in 2007 I was made redundant; and unfortunately as a contractor this meant that I did not qualify for a redundancy package, so I moved my attention to designing and building websites. At the same time, we had started changing our lifestyle to become "greener" and more self-sufficient.

However, we were becoming disenchanted with the UK. My wife's parents owned a small farm in central France, although the actual activity of farming had ceased a decade ago when they retired. My mother-in-law became ill and passed away, and as my father-in-law's health had been deteriorating also, we decided this could be the ideal opportunity to sell up and move to France. Not only would we be able to offer assistance to my father-in-law, but this would be our chance of becoming fully self-sufficient (or at least, as self-sufficient as possible in a modern world).

Our friends had mixed reactions to this plan. Whilst the majority were supportive, saying things like "Ooh, I wish we could do that!" others were dismissive. To those who asked "Why France?" the answer was simple. "Because that's where the farm is!"

Being "green" or ecological is seen as expensive. Our aim is to prove that this need not be the case. Not only would we be ecological, we would be economically ecological!

By the way, I don't want to have to keep writing "father-in-law", so henceforth I shall refer to him as "the aged FIL". Whilst we're on the subject, I shall refer to my wife as "LSS" from this point onwards. And in case you're wondering, it means "Long-Suffering Spouse." Although there are occasions when I wonder whether the term should not refer to me instead. Other abbreviations will no doubt follow, being used to protect innocent parties involved.

The Property

L OCATED on the very border of Loir-et-Cher, the farm itself is around thirty hectares (or 74 acres) in size, shaped like the letter "W", and its redeeming feature, as far as we were concerned, was that it had a house at either end, a kilometre apart. We had no objection to being closer to the aged FIL, but we didn't actually want to live with him. He can be a cantankerous old so-and-so. He lives in one house, and we will live in the other.

Now, I need to mention at this point that the aged FIL's house is something which Dickens would have had no trouble recognising. The roof tends to leak when it rains, and the walls are not exactly what I would call solid. Apart from that, there are only four items worth describing.

These are:

1. Electricity. Badly in need of upgrading.

2. Cold running water. The mod cons stop there. There's no hot water unless you boil it yourself in a kettle on the gas stove. There's no bathroom, but there is a:

3. Hand-made concrete kitchen sink. This is where the cold tap water supply is, and is also where the washing-up is done. There is also a:

4. Lavatory. This is, of course, outside. At the furthest end of the house. It's simply a hole in the ground, covered by a bench with a plastic toilet seat. It does have rough wooden walls and a corrugated iron roof. You don't want

to spend too much time in there, especially in winter, because it's extremely draughty.

As regards personal hygiene, what's that? If you want to wash, use (3) above. Not quite the ideal conditions for an aged person, hmm? Actually, not quite the ideal conditions for a non-aged person either, in my opinion.

Since farming ceased, the land has been returning to its natural flora, namely mixed woodland. The soil isn't much good for growing anything else, if I'm honest. In fact Sologne used to be an area of swamps. When the Romans travelled through Gaul they passed through this area. One of the little lakes nearby is called "Caesar's Lake", and rumour has it that it was dug by the Romans so that it could be stocked with fish in order to feed the passing troops. I don't think Julius himself wielded a spade though.

The house in which we planned to live was built in the nineteenth century, and, discounting the spiders, had been empty for some thirty years. There is an electricity supply, although the wiring is badly in need of upgrading. It's also three-phase, so that will be an entirely new learning curve for me. There's a well, although personally I wouldn't drink the pale orange water unless it was boiled first. Gravity seems to work fine. And that's it. No bathroom. No telephone. No running water. It's even more basic than the aged FIL's house mentioned above. With a couple of small advantages though; the roof doesn't leak, and the walls are more solid.

We will need to:

- Install a rainwater harvesting system together with guttering (there are no gutters on the house)

- Start a garden (to provide us with food, obviously)

- Obtain a drinking-water supply (also for domestic use, like washing!)

- Sort out some central heating (there's an old wood-burning range in the kitchen but that's all)

- Improve the electricity supply (supplemented or hopefully replaced with solar panels)

- Install a domestic hot water supply (again solar thermal, preferably)

- Re-plaster and redecorate (the plaster is falling off the walls in places)

- Install a bathroom (there is no lavatory or washing facilities unless you count the kitchen sink)

So we have lots to do in order to transform the living accommodation into something a bit more modern. The goal is to do this as ecologically as possible, but at the same time using modern methods. However, to make this a bit more interesting, the entire principle behind this project is to renovate the property by using as little money as possible. The main reason for this is that selling a house during a recession generally means the amount of money left over is extremely limited! And of course the self-sufficiency aspect will play a major role;

we'll be growing our own food as much as possible. We will be implementing the three "R's" to their utmost:

- Reduce!

- Re-use!

- Recycle!

Our budget for this project? £10 000. Or €12 000 in continental money. Can it be done? We'll certainly try!

(Actually this budget is not entirely accurate, because a few months after we arrived, the aged FIL's mood improved, and he offered to pay for the installation of a borehole. But getting the water from the borehole to the house would be up to us).

As far as earning a living was concerned, my linguistic lack of French would pose a problem. However, if we were going to be renovating the property without spending lots of cash, this meant that I would have to do the renovating myself. And if I was going to be working full-time on the renovations, I couldn't very well get outside employment at the same time, now could I? Fortunately LSS is completely bilingual in French and English, so she planned on utilising these skills in translation, teaching English, and possibly assisting businesses with customer service (her other strong point). When she wasn't otherwise occupied with helping me with the renovations, of course!

The Move

OF course, as is usually the case when one is trying to sell a property, it was the wrong time to sell. The housing market was at a low point, and we were let down by a string of buyers in succession. After eight long months we were finally successful.

By this time, the aged FIL was in hospital. He'd had a stomach bug which caused him to lose his appetite, so he'd simply decided to stop eating. This of course meant that he grew increasingly weaker, until finally he was unable to pick himself up when he fell over. (He was fairly unsteady on his pins even before this). He spent an uncomfortable night on the kitchen floor, and was found the following morning by M&O. (There's another abbreviation for you. They're a retired couple who are in charge of the local hunt. They rent the hunting rights to the property, and also did the aged FIL's shopping before we finally arrived. All in all, a couple of Good Eggs).

Just to make matters worse, he had also decided he didn't want to speak to LSS any more, and was refusing to take her telephone calls. Of course this meant she was starting to have second thoughts about the whole moving-to-France idea. But with the house no longer ours, and the furniture already in transit, we really had no alternative.

As the aged FIL's house would be uninhabited, we decided to commence our project by staying in that house until such time as we could make the other building habitable.

Having finally dropped off the keys to our old house at the estate agents, we left the UK around lunchtime. I travelled on my Honda Pan European ST1100 motorcycle, following the instructions from my Garmin GPS. LSS followed me in her car with the cat as a travelling companion. We took it easy, stopping for a break every hour or so and using the back roads in order to avoid motorway tolls. Rouen proved interesting as we had to drive around a bit to find a petrol station which was open. After filling up, we were inadvertently separated by a roundabout, so I pulled over to the side of the road to wait. Fortunately it was not yet dark and the terrain was fairly flat, so almost immediately LSS noticed I was no longer ahead of her. Frantically looking around, she spotted me waiting in the distance, on a different road, with the two of us being separated by several fields. We finally arrived at our destination at one o'clock in the morning, and the only one who was not tired from the trip was the cat. My odometer showed the trip to be just under 700km. Not even worth mentioning, really.

The Diary Starts: March

S ETTLING in, we start removing the clutter of years, and our furniture arrives.

Saturday 24th

Despite getting to bed in the small hours, we were up early to empty the car. Then we did a bit of food shopping in the closest large town, Lamotte Beuvron.

It was now time to visit our new residence. The plan is that when all our furniture arrives, it will be stored in the barn until such time as we have renovated the existing rooms. Ah, yes, but that means the barn needs to be empty first!

Unfortunately the aged FIL is a hoarder. Nothing – and I mean nothing - gets thrown away. We decided that one of the outbuildings (which seemed to have been a rabbit pen at one stage of its life) will be used to house anything metallic until such time as we can sell it to a scrap metal dealer. Another outbuilding turned out to be inhabited by a very surprised barn owl. This building was re-purposed to house all the bits of wood until we have a board meeting to decide what to do with it all.

Underneath the pile of junk lurked something large and heavy-looking. It was a horse-drawn cart. LSS and I managed to drag it out of the barn without dismantling too many walls on the way, and parked it in a field. Maybe we'll sell it on Ebay. "Offered for auction: horse-drawn cart. One previous lady owner. Genuine French woodworm supplied free of charge." Or maybe not. It may just fall apart on its own. It actually had a metal name-tag nailed to one of the shafts, bearing the name of LSS's grandmother.

With the barn finally empty we levelled the dirt floor as much as we could, filling in the larger rabbit holes. The earth was then covered with a couple of large tarpaulins which we'd had the foresight to bring, ready for our furniture which is due to arrive next Tuesday.

Upon returning to the aged FIL's house, I spied a couple of old bathtubs in a field. They had originally been used for watering cattle. We took a closer look and managed to find one in fairly good condition. We cleaned off the worst of the dirt and rust, and set it up in the middle of the garden. LSS whittled a bathplug out of a large cork and voila – an open-air bathroom! We heated some water on the gas stove and managed to rinse off all the woodworm dust.

LSS had the brilliant idea of taking a photograph of me enjoying a bath au naturel in more ways than one; fortunately for me the camera battery had gone flat.

Some slight improvements are needed though; we need a bit more water! The bath was emptied by the simple method of turning it on its side – oh, weren't the earthworms surprised! We then added about twenty litres of water to the tub; it will be left in the sunshine all day tomorrow to warm up.

Sunday 25th

We've decided to take Sundays off; with the amount of work which needs to be done we're going to need one day a week free of renovating! We visited the aged FIL in hospital; he was his normal crotchety self. He didn't explain why he had refused LSS's telephone calls.

When we returned, the water in the bath which had been left in the garden all day wasn't very warm. Mind you, it hadn't collected too many drowned insects, which was a pleasant surprise. But I did have another cunning plan. In our possession is a black plastic twenty-litre jerry can. This had also been filled with water and left in full sunshine. It heated up its contents quite nicely, which meant that we only needed to boil two kettles on the gas stove in order to have a nice hot bath.

Monday 26th

Following our board meeting, it has been decided that the wood which is currently residing in one of the outhouses will contribute to the fuel supply for the wood stove. It's full of woodworm so basically can't be used for anything else. There was a wardrobe in the bedroom which we were hoping to use, but as we tried to move it, it fell apart. Oops. Oh well.

There are quite a few old wooden chairs as well; the woodworm (or possibly termites, not too sure which) have had a field day on these too – but have been very particular to eat the bottom of only ONE of the legs on each chair. Very odd indeed. The chairs feed the wood stove too, because we become tired of having to place a brick under one leg of each chair to maintain the equilibrium. Two replacement chairs were brought from the aged FIL's house. These are in slightly better condition.

The bedroom and lounge are finally empty of junk, and we're able to get our first view of the lounge walls; the plaster is coming away in sheets so that's yet another job for the to-do list. Tired, dirty, but happy, we retire to the other house and have another well-deserved wash in the open air.

Tuesday 27th

I hate waiting. If I ever have an appointment somewhere, I'm always at least ten minutes early. If someone is coming to visit me at a certain time, I'm always on tenterhooks from about twenty minutes beforehand. So today is not a good day; the furniture is due to arrive. Sort of around lunchtime. Maybe.

LSS busied herself vacuuming the walls and ceilings in both rooms; the spiders had been amusing themselves by doing their own decorating here.

At this point we discovered that the mobile phone reception at the property is – practically – nil. I finally manage to get a signal by moving into the middle of a field, and standing on one leg, with the phone held horizontally. The missed calls were from the driver of the removals lorry who had left a message that they had stopped to have lunch and should be with us by one o'clock.

At a quarter past one, the mobile phone rang again and then cut off as soon as I answered the call. After lots of manoeuvring to find the best signal, I finally managed to understand that it was the driver of the removals lorry again, saying that he was uncertain of the exact location of the property. I had compiled a detailed map and emailed this to the office with the credit card details – but, of course, this information had not been given to the driver. I ended up driving the car to the junction with the main road, where I parked it on the verge. I then dashed out into the middle of the road, waving, as soon as I saw a lorry appear over the brow of the hill. The first three were very surprised, having nothing to do with furniture deliveries at all.

But finally the Pickfords lorry was parked at the entrance to the barn, and unloading could commence.

Everything was finally stored in the barn and we waved goodbye to the crew at around four o'clock. Another telephone call was then received by LSS; the aged FIL is being released from hospital on the 29th; so it's time to vacate his premises and move the cat to her proper home, namely, here!

Wednesday 28th

We visit Salbris to do some shopping. I'm particularly anxious to buy some anti-woodworm product to treat the beams in the bedroom; if you tap them, you're rewarded with a cloud of dust. Fortunately they're oak and very thick, so any damage should only be superficial. Still, it's worth making sure that the only woodworm remaining are dead ones.

I was able to purchase some stuff containing Fipronil; strangely enough it's the same stuff used against ticks and fleas for the cat. Hmm. I wonder which is cheaper?

We have also gathered together a collection of empty two-litre plastic fizzy drink bottles. These will be filled at the aged FIL's kitchen sink on a daily basis, and brought here to provide a supply of drinking water (and bath water, until we can figure out how the well works).

Our first night in our new home!

Thursday 29th

(Alternative title: Everything you wanted to know about French Supermarket Petrol Stations but were afraid to ask...)

These are usually the cheapest places at which one can buy petrol. This low price, however, has its disadvantages. If you arrive before opening hours, you have to wait patiently until the little hand moves to one minute past the official opening hour. At this point the cashier-attendant suddenly appears from nowhere, and ambles slowly into the little kiosk, where he presses the magic button and the petrol pump display windows flicker into life.

The other disadvantage with the Supermarket petrol station involves the actual payment for your petrol – especially if you don't have a French bank card, a *Carte Bleu*, (which means you can use the automated pump). What about using foreign cards? Ha! Let zem eat cake! *Non.* It simply ejects the card from the slot as though it doesn't like the taste.

So you have to drive forward to the cashier. This is when you discover that when the cashier kiosks were first built, the Renault 2CV was the only car available in France, and the kiosk design has not changed in the intervening years. From any other car you have to lie down on the passenger seat, and extend your double-jointed arm downwards through the car window, then upwards into the little tunnel at the kiosk, in order to put your card into the machine which the cashier is usually holding just out of your reach. Entering your card pin number involves further contortions, and if you wear spectacles you normally end up with them dangling upside-down from one ear. None of this is helped by the fact that the cashier kiosk is always on the left-hand side of the car. Of course, for a left-hand drive vehicle this is fine. But for our right-hand drive vehicle it's a problem.

Actually, I say it's fine. Well it isn't. I've seen drivers of left-hand drive vehicles struggling too. Fortunately LSS is generally in the passenger seat, but even then she has to fold her arm into sundry different positions in order to pay for the petrol, no matter how close I can bring the vehicle to the side of the building.

The other option of course is to leave your vehicle where it is once you have filled the tank, and walk to the kiosk. The height of the window means you have to crouch down to pay, but this certainly makes things easier. However, even this method has a disadvantage. When you have paid and return to your car, the vehicle next to you shoots forward to the cashier, blocking you in. And inevitably the driver will be a long-lost cousin of the cashier, leading to a long conversation.

We fetched the aged FIL from the hospital this afternoon. I sensed an air of disapproval from him about my driving; maybe I wasn't going fast enough. Or maybe it was just that he was unsettled about being in the left-hand seat of a right-hand drive car. He didn't say a word though, which is probably just as well as I probably wouldn't have understood him anyway. A couple of days ago one of LSS' cousins had brought us an old wheelchair. It used to belong to the aged FIL's brother until he passed away, and she said we would probably need it. She was right. She obviously knew more about the way the French hospital system works than we did.

(I had to pump up the tyres first though, as they were a bit flat).

April

S ADLY the aged FIL takes up most of our time. The weather becomes unseasonably cold, but at least we manage to have a telephone line installed.

Wednesday 4th
The gap in diary entries was due to circumstances entirely beyond our control.

The truth of the matter is that we are spending the majority of our time looking after the aged FIL. We jump out of bed in the morning and drive to the other house, get him out of bed, take him to the lavatory, and feed him. Then we put him back to bed, drive back to our house, manage to do one or two things and then it's time to drive back to the other house to get him out of bed, take him to the lavatory, and feed him lunch. Then we put him back to bed, drive back to our house, manage to do one or two things, (have you noticed a sense of *déjà vu* yet?) and then it's time to drive back to the other house to get him out of bed, take him to the lavatory, and feed him dinner. Then we put him back to bed, drive back to our house, and pretty much collapse with exhaustion.

In addition we need to do his shopping as well, which also involves visiting the chemist for all his prescriptions (which literally fills two shopping bags, I'm not joking). Unfortunately things can't continue in this vein; we just don't have the time to do anything else, let alone get on with the renovation of our house.

In fact, now that we think about it, the hospital in Vierzon has not done a good job at all with regard to after-sales service. The aged FIL was simply discharged. As he can hardly walk, it turned out to be exceedingly fortunate that we had brought our own wheelchair, as no hospital-owned wheelchairs were in evidence anywhere. Or indeed offered. LSS's cousin obviously knew this would happen. No doctor or nurse came to have a chat with us about what care he should have at home. No word about any special diet. No advice about what assistance is available. Nothing.

LSS was so annoyed about this she wrote a two-page letter of complaint to the director of the hospital, expressing her displeasure with the way the discharge was handled. Pay attention now, because you'll need this information later: she mentioned the letter to the aged FIL. He was in complete agreement; this was not the way he should have been treated. He then warmed to the idea, said he was actually quite annoyed with the hospital, and instructed LSS to mention this in the letter also.

On the renovation front, all I have managed to do so far is to clear away the piled-up earth from the side of the house. This revealed lots of spalled and missing bricks at the foundation level. It's not a good thing to have soil up against the wall of a building; it transmits damp. Especially if there aren't any gutters. There's no damp-proof course either; fortunately it's a double-thickness wall otherwise I suspect it would have collapsed by now.

As far as lavatory facilities are concerned, these were non-existent when we moved in. No, actually that's not quite true.

There was a purpose-built brick outhouse adjacent to the barn, with a plastic toilet seat fitted to a concrete bench, with a plastic bucket underneath. Goodness knows where the aged FIL used to empty it. I carried the bucket into the woods and gave it a decent burial.

Our aim is to purchase a proper composting toilet, which would be installed together with a proper shower, bath and sink in a proper bathroom. The barn adjoining the house would be subdivided into four rooms; two bedrooms, a study, and a bathroom. However, the first thing which needed to be done for this subdivision would be the installation of a proper floor; and it would be some time before work could be started on this particular phase of the project. More important phases were the provision of potable water, and insulation against the oncoming winter!

So until such time as we could obtain a proper composting toilet, there was really only one option available; namely, to construct a latrine. In a convenient glade in the woods adjoining the farmhouse, I dug a hole. Over this hole was placed a wooden chair with its seat missing. The recycled plastic toilet seat from the disused "outhouse" was then fixed to the chair. An ex-army poncho provided a screen to the front, and trees screened the other three sides. After every visit, a thin layer of soil is placed over the deposit until the hole is full, and a new hole is then dug adjacent to the old one. The piece of turf which was carefully put to one side when the hole was excavated is then replaced, with the result that the hole disappears entirely.

The temperature is still below zero at night, and with no insulation in the house it's pretty chilly! There were two broken window panes which I covered with pieces of hardboard as a temporary fix. The aged wood stove is proving to be a real blessing.

Mind you, on a positive note, by using the aged FIL's phone we have managed to place an order for our own phone line. This came as a bundle with unlimited Internet (hooray!) and television. We won't actually be using the latter service, as our television is still in a box somewhere in the barn. When it is finally extricated, we only intend using it for watching DVD's. It's an old analogue model so can't receive the modern French digital signal anyway – this will come in handy when they come around to enquire why we don't have a license. There is a television aerial on the roof at La Darnoire, but it's not connected to anything. We decided to go with Orange as the phone supplier (they took over from France Telecom). We have also requested a letter box from the Post Office.

Cat appears extremely happy and is proving to be a hit with the local mouse population. Literally. But she still eats her dinner and is not putting on weight. She must have hollow legs.

Friday 6th

Two young engineers from Orange paid us a visit today! They said they had connected up the telephone line, but it was not yet ready for use. Once they had gone we wandered down the road to see how they had installed it. The neighbouring property has a telephone line, so the junction box is at the entrance to their farm, a distance of about 400m from us.

The engineers had used the existing concrete EDF electricity pylons, and had simply strung the telephone line from pole to pole. Not very well, either. The cable was tangled in some tree branches next to the road (these are the branches that are regularly pruned by EDF's branch-chopping machines). The last section of the line (furthest from our house) is simply trailing along the ground. We can't even call them yet to tell them to come back to fix it properly! Besides, they would have knocked off for the weekend anyway.

Saturday 7th

There's not much progress to report; the aged FIL is still taking up much of our time. We did manage to plant the tree seedlings which we brought over from the UK; four elders, two saplings which could possibly be peach trees – at least the leaves look like peach leaves, but we can't be sure as neither LSS nor I can remember planting peach trees - and something which could possibly be a cherry tree when it grows up.

I also made a start at cleaning up the "orchard". This is simply a row of a few trees in a small clearing in the woodland. They had been planted about fifteen years ago and then abandoned. The tallest is about a metre high. None of them are as tall as they should be - which is not that surprising as they were choked with weeds and brambles. They're looking a lot tidier now. I think two of them are walnuts. There are a couple of apple trees, and two dead sticks. And an anthill.

For the first time we boiled some water using the kitchen wood burner – it came in extremely handy for our bath in the garden! We brought the bath here from the other house in the back of the old Renault 5. LSS inherited this vehicle from the late MIL and it is coming in handy for a farm runabout. I set up a couple of my old army ponchos in order to screen the bath from the prevailing winds.

Sunday 8th
Could it possibly be Sunday again? Where does the time go?

We went to a restaurant in Salbris with three of LSS's cousins as a treat. They had not seen LSS for a very, very long time. Twenty years? Something like that.

Monday 9th
Today was the day we attacked the pantry! Yes, we have a pantry, a small room used for storing food. It's right next to the kitchen, obviously, but strangely the floor level is lower than that of the kitchen so you have to step down into it.

Nobody thought about doing anything about the height of the doorway though. Previous French residents here must have been tiny. It's about 1.6 metres high, which means I have to remember to duck when entering the room. Even LSS has to be careful, and she's shorter than I am.

The thing is, the shelves were attached to the wall by means of wooden brackets. And not only the shelves, but the wooden brackets too had all succumbed to the dreaded woodworm. (Why do they call it woodworm? It's a beetle!) Anyway, all the old shelving and the brackets were removed with the aid of a hammer. This was probably overkill; I suspect they would have fallen off by themselves if I'd left them alone for much longer.

LSS used the vacuum cleaner to remove the spiders and cobwebs from the ceiling. It's a wet-and-dry vacuum cleaner, which is probably just as well. Mind you, I don't think the spiders were particularly concerned about which type of vacuum cleaner it was.

Tuesday 10th
The aged FIL is taken back to hospital for a scheduled operation. We won't be visiting him every day; two hours' travelling is a bit much. We may finally get some work done.

He has diabetic feet and is due to have a sort of balloon inserted into an artery in one leg in order to improve the circulation. The official name is a "stent". However, he insists that he doesn't have diabetes.

"Yes you do; it's why you have diabetic feet."

"No, I don't have diabetes. I just have a problem with something the doctor said was blood sugar."

"Yes, that's called diabetes."

"Oh, I didn't know that. I thought I had a problem with blood sugar."

"Yes, you do."

"Hah! You see! It's not diabetes!"

(Repeat until bored).

Wednesday 11th
We have decided that today is rabbit poo day. No, you did read that correctly. You see, the late MIL used to keep rabbits. (Vegetarians look away now).

These fluffy bunnies were for food, not for pets.

(Right, vegetarians, you can start reading again).

Whenever the cages were cleaned out, all the detritus was just dumped in a pile in the garden. Over the years this gradually turned into a very dark brown, rich compost. There must be several tons of it. Well, we decided instead of just leaving it there, we'd dig it into our garden. I managed to start the tractor, and as there was a large metal transport box already attached to the rear, simply used this to carry two 44-gallon drums full of rabbit-dropping compost back to our house. The now-empty drums will become our new compost bins. And every time we visit the other house, we'll bring back a large tub of the stuff. There's no point in wasting a trip, is there?

LSS started washing the kitchen walls, which are brown in colour. I didn't say the paint was brown, I said the walls were brown in colour. I think the paint used to be white originally. The ceiling is brown too. I have no idea how we're going to clean it sufficiently before painting it; I suspect even my industrial-sized tub of sugar soap won't be enough. I do have a Karcher pressure washer though...

Thursday 12th

The telephone and Internet are now working! WE'RE ONLINE AGAIN! Without having to use a dial-up modem at the aged FIL's house!

The telephone line here is still trailing along the ground though; Orange/France Telecom haven't yet fixed that.

As the morning was bright and sunny, we decided to work on clearing up some of the front garden which was overgrown with nettles and brambles. It's so nice not to have to look after the aged FIL for a while!

As the afternoon clouded over, an Orange/France Telecom engineer arrived. He immediately spotted the problem; (it's not difficult to see, remember the line is trailing along the ground). However, that's not his department. He's actually come to ensure the internet is up and running (it is). He connects his laptop, fiddles around with it a bit, and exclaims (in French, of course): "Ah, ha! You could have a line speed of *deux mega!*"

"Great!" we enthuse.

"*Mais oui.* But, if I set it to two Mbps[1] it won't be stable. Because of the distance from the exchange it would be best if I set it to one Mbps."

"Well, as long as we're online, I can't see we'll notice much of a difference between one and two Mbps."

"No, no, you're right there. However I will need to report back to head office that you only have a one Mbps connection."

"Fine, fine, whatever you say." (Little did we know...)

Friday 13th

I cut some more wood for the wood burner. Oh it's so nice to be able to use a chainsaw again! Which is a weird thing to say. Unless you happen to be a Forestry Officer who hasn't worked in Forestry for over twenty years. Yes, that would be me.

The other good news is that the aged FIL will be staying in hospital until at least Tuesday next week. Who says Friday the thirteenth is unlucky?

---

[1]Mbps = megabits per second, an indication of internet transfer speed

LSS takes the opportunity to catch up on some of the clothes washing. Unfortunately the aged FIL's equally-aged washing machine is just about to expire. It works fine until it needs to either fill or empty itself; at which point it decides it just can't be bothered and leaks water all over the kitchen floor.

Saturday 14th

A spot of grocery shopping in the morning resulted in my buying a couple of pieces of meat which I thought would be ideal barbecue material. As it's turned out to be a nice sunny day, this will be what we'll have for supper. Our first barbecue in France!

LSS has been busy trying to organise some "home help". Basically this is done by a company which specialises in looking after elderly people. Most of the costs will be met by the aged FIL's insurance policy, but he'll still need to contribute something. He's not too happy about the idea but LSS has pointed out that we didn't come to France solely with the aim of looking after him; we don't mind helping out, but full-time carers we are not!

I spent the afternoon cutting through the stems of the ivy which is covering the outbuilding intended to be our future garage. Although ivy on a building does look attractive, it's not very good for the brickwork. And this particular ivy has decided it likes the interior of the building as well, so it has to go. Chopping through the base should cause the majority of the vegetation to die off, at which time it should be easier to remove. I'll tackle the root system at a later date. At the same time, I pruned the grapevines which are being smothered by the aforementioned ivy. It's probably a bit late in the year to prune grapevines, but too bad.

With the day's labour complete, I lit the barbecue. But as soon as I put the meat on the grid, it started to rain. However, we're made of tougher stuff than that. LSS dashed indoors to fetch some auxiliary equipment, and I finished cooking our supper under the protective covering of a fetchingly-coloured purple ladies' umbrella.

Sunday 15th

Right, who left the refrigerator door open? It feels more like February than mid-April; it's freezing cold!

We visited the aged FIL in hospital in the afternoon, and were looking forward to getting back to our aged wood stove in the kitchen in order to warm up.

Unfortunately, this time we were unable to light it success-fully. Smoke started billowing out of every orifice (even some we did not know it had) and the only solution was to fling open all the doors and windows so that we could see what we were doing. I grabbed the barbecue tongs and rushed the smouldering bits of wood outside. I suspect the stove itself has passed its use-by date but it could just be something as simple as a sooty chimney. Another job for LSS's list tomorrow: find a chimney sweep. We decide it will be warmer in bed, so retire early.

Monday 16th

LSS called a chimney sweep who promised to call back and didn't. I'm starting to wonder whether we ought to get some huskies.

"Let's move to France," LSS had said. "It's warmer there," she had said. Humph.

In the end we drove into town to visit LSS's aged aunt and beg the use of her hot shower. We did stop off at the supermarket on the way in order to buy an apple tart as a bribe. This was quite successful because she is particularly fond of apple tarts. But as punishment for trying to bribe her, she force-fed us lots of pancakes.

This turned out to be A Good Thing. We happened to notice a bathroom scale in the aged aunt's bathroom, and tried it out. I had noticed my trousers were becoming slightly loose. Ah-ha! LSS has lost four kilograms since coming to France, and I've lost nine. This lifestyle of running around after the aged FIL has some use then!

Tuesday 17th

Today we visited the village of Brinon in order to meet the bank manager of the local HSBC Bank to get an account opened for me. Oh my goodness, the amount of paperwork required! They need lots of documents which we're getting together in order to hand them in next week. LSS was finally able to find a local chimney sweep and has requested an urgent visit tomorrow. I think that chattering her teeth during the telephone call was a bit of overkill, but it may have the desired effect. I will be paying close attention to how the chimney is swept so that I can do it myself in future when necessary.

Unfortunately the lack of a working wood stove means we have to sit in the kitchen wearing several jumpers and jackets. We have plugged in a small electric fan heater, and this has managed to raise the inside temperature to around 8 degrees

Centigrade. For entertainment we watch the electricity meter whizzing around merrily, and I annoy LSS by quoting her.

"'Let's move to France,' she said. 'It's warmer there,' she said."

Tomorrow we're off to Vierzon hospital to visit the aged FIL and also to meet the doctor who apparently has important MATTERS TO DISCUSS. They refused to give any further details over the telephone, so we'll have to wait and see what it's about.

We're still really living out of cardboard boxes. The main barn is attached to the house, and that's where all our furniture and cardboard boxes are stored. Obviously when we need something, the box is inevitably at the bottom of all the others. Anyway, LSS decided she wanted some particular item and disappeared into the barn to look for it. We knew which box it was in.

Twenty minutes later, LSS had still not reappeared. So I wandered out to see what was happening. As I got to the door I heard:

Rustle, rustle, rustle, creak, rustle.

"*Merde.*"

Rustle, creak, creak, rustle, rustle.

"*Merde alors!*" (plus some other French which I didn't quite understand)

Rustle creak rustle creak rustle (these I deduced were the sounds of cardboard boxes being moved and opened).

Rustle rustle rustle creak...

"*Merde!*"

Rustle rustle...

And then in a rising crescendo:

"Oh you great big PILE OF POO!!"

At which point I collapsed laughing.

With no television, we tend to go to bed a lot earlier - usually around 9 p.m. when it gets dark. It's too cold to just sit about! Generally we wake up at around 6.30 a.m. and get up soon afterwards, because the cat is inevitably jumping up and down asking "Where's my breakfast?" Unfortunately I haven't managed to train her properly yet to switch on the coffee machine and fry the bacon, but I have High Hopes.

Her understanding is that we want Mouse to eat, as we generally find one on the doorstep as a present. When we moved in, we found an old ragged duvet which we decided to use to wrap up the lemon tree and bell peppers (which we'd brought with us from the UK) as protection against the frost.

LSS started unwrapping it this morning, and I heard a shriek: "AAARGH! A RAT!!" There was definitely a long-tailed rodent scurrying up and down inside the duvet, so I called the cat. She ambled over, wondering what all the fuss was about - until she saw the movement, upon which she pounced where she thought it was. The rodent immediately shot out of one of the holes in the side of the duvet, and headed for the hills, with the cat in close pursuit.

At this point it became evident it wasn't a rat, because it was running like a little kangaroo, and had a long tail with a white bushy end. It was a garden dormouse. Anyway, it climbed a fence post and sat on top, shouting with rage. It had a white face with black markings, exactly like a little bandit. I caught up the cat and removed her from the area, leaving the dormouse to scurry away into the ivy. Poor little thing!

Wednesday 18th

Success! We have a working wood stove again. The problem was partially the chimney and partially the wood stove. I now know how to dismantle this particular chimney pipe for cleaning purposes, and how to semi-dismantle the stove in order to scrape caked soot from its inner workings. (Note to self: Buy some chimney sweeping brushes.)

As for the hospital doctor's meeting, the MATTERS TO DISCUSS was not a meeting with the doctor at all. It was a meeting between LSS, myself (as a not-yet-French-speaking-observer), the aged FIL, a doctor, and THREE senior administrative staff of the hospital.

They were basically highly upset about the letter which LSS had written to the director, and took great pains to point out that it was, basically, all her own fault.

"What? You didn't tell me whether he needed any sort of special care or not," LSS stated.

"You should have asked," was the reply, with nodding heads.

"He wasn't offered the option of a wheelchair," LSS said.

"You should have asked," they said, with folded arms.

"I wasn't told whether he should have a special diet or not," LSS said.

"You should have asked," was the reply, with wagging fingers.

"How was I supposed to know what questions I should have asked?" asked LSS.

"You should have asked," they chorused, triumphantly.

Now, do you remember when I told you to pay attention earlier? Because at this point the aged FIL interjected that he knew nothing about any letter, did not at any time discuss the writing of said unknown letter, and even after he had not actually not discussed the non-writing of the non-letter, he wanted it to be understood that he didn't actually agree that it should be sent at all. "Gee, thanks for the support, Dad," muttered LSS under her breath. At least I presume that's what she said. It was, after all, in French. And rather short. And I don't think you can actually translate *that* word as "support".

So THAT was a complete waste of time. But still, the fact that the hospital staff at Vierzon had decided to bring so many staff to a meeting with the hope that LSS would be overwhelmed by superior numbers was obviously an admission of guilt.

Oh – and if a member of staff at the Vierzon hospital happens to read this – Please. Next time you want to try and intimidate someone, take the trouble to find out a bit more about that person first. LSS is not a simple village person who has stayed in the same village for all her life. She's lived in another country for twenty years, and is not likely to be intimidated when faced with superior numbers of opponents; in fact this has the opposite effect as it presents more of a challenge, which she enjoys. So there.

We're still researching the best place to buy DIY stuff for the house. So far, we have a short list: Castorama, Leroy Merlin, and a place called Weldom in Aubigny. We also visited a place called "Point P" but were not that impressed – it seems to cater more for the trade than the public, and the prices were galactic (a degree higher than astronomical). Perhaps the "P" stands for "Pricey".

We're also looking for somewhere we can order a replacement wood stove. I'm considering one with a back boiler so it can supply some of the domestic hot water. We found a website of a place based in Neung-sur-Beuvron and paid them a visit. Eek! Talk about high prices. Not our cup of tea at all.

Thursday 19th

Today was a strange sort of day. We fetched the aged FIL from Vierzon hospital, and once again there was no communication regarding his post-operative care. And no, we didn't ask. We're starting to think that this is the norm for the French medical system.

LSS received a letter notifying her that her bank account is finally open. Unfortunately she is unable to transfer any money into it because she doesn't have an electronic card reader from her UK bank. So if you're reading this, have a NatWest bank account, and want to do an online transfer from the UK, make sure you have an electronic card reader before you leave. As for me, I can transfer funds quite happily because I'm with First Direct in the UK. That is to say, I would be able to transfer funds quite happily, but am currently unable to do this because I still haven't managed to get a French bank account.

Further research into a wood stove with back boiler has taken place. We like the idea increasingly each time we discuss it. It can hopefully provide domestic hot water with enough left over to heat a couple of radiators (especially in the bedroom which is a bit cold!) After all, there are thirty hectares of woodland so we shouldn't run short of fuel!

Today I received an email reply from a UK supplier of wood stoves. I had seen on their website that they had wood stoves with back boilers, and I wanted to know whether it was possible to have one delivered to France. Unfortunately this information was not forthcoming. Instead the email was rather snooty.

They said (and I quote):

"I WANT A BOILER STOVE! Waste of time and a very expensive installation cost which takes a long long time to re-pay. The Royal Collage(sic) of Engineers announced in January 2012 that they were recognising that plumbers are currently not trained or experienced enough for the eco technology ie installation of boiler stoves. We recognised this several years ago and withdrew our boiler stoves from the market. Translated plumbers were a hit and miss for installation and we were finding some plumbers taking £2000 to £3000 to leave with a plumbing system that did not work, not just from our stoves but from all boiler stoves on the market. We feel chances of finding an installer who can actually fit it is minimal as the knowledge has been lost over a generation, young plumbers are not up to the technology and the cost of fitting outweighs the benefit of any hot water produced. Just go for the largest woodburner you can install without a boiler."

I replied that it was a pity they no longer supplied boiler stoves. I wasn't too sure what a translated plumber was, but as I would be installing the stove myself, the cost of fitting would have been zero.

Unfortunately this reply was not taken kindly at all. The answer I received was fairly insulting, casting aspersions on my ability. I did try to find the email so I could quote the reply in its entirety, but then remembered I was so annoyed at the time that I just deleted it.

LSS has written a letter to Honda France enquiring about getting a *Certificate de Conformité* for my Honda Pan European ST1100 motorcycle. This document is apparently needed before you can get a *"Carte Grise"* which is the name of the official French vehicle registration document. Whilst she was in the mood, she also wrote a letter to Hyundai so that she can get her car registered here as well.

Oh, and Orange/France Telecom turned up to look at the problem with the line. Let's see, this is the ... um ... yes, third engineer they've sent.

Unfortunately they haven't fully explained the problem to him. He can see that the line is trailing along the ground; however, as the only equipment they've given him is a short ladder and a wooden stick, there's not much he can do about fixing it to the EDF pylons which are at least twice the height of his ladder. Dejectedly, he throws away the wooden stick, replaces the ladder in his van and leaves. You couldn't make it up.

Friday 20th

Orange/France Telecom turn up again. This is Engineer Number Four. Once again it's a solitary engineer, but this time he has a proper high-lift cherry-picker vehicle. I suspect he's the Divisional Manager because he does a thorough job; undoing the work of engineers One and Two and re-doing it properly by fixing metal extension arms to the EDF pylons so that the telephone line avoids the tree branches. This is handy because when EDF come past once a year with their tree-branch cutting machine, it would have been a certainty that our telephone line would have been chopped into little pieces in several places.

It took him a couple of hours to do the job, and when he'd finished and was driving off, we ran out into the roadway to tearfully wave our handkerchiefs in gratitude at the departing vehicle.

"Thank goodness THAT's finally resolved," LSS said.

"Yes, hopefully it will be a very long time before we need to deal with Orange again," I replied. I should have kept my mouth shut.

Other than that, our research on where we can get DIY stuff is proving to be very annoying. Shopping for DIY stuff in France is not simple. Unlike in Britain where companies have websites where you can add stuff to a basket, click Checkout and it tells you how much delivery will cost, this is not the case here.

Yes, all right, we live in the middle of nowhere, but still, this is the twenty-first century after all! Take Leroy Merlin's website as an example. Half the stuff we wanted was not available to buy online. LSS called them to enquire about delivery charges, and was told that it all depended on how many pallets were in the order. Fair enough, I suppose, but the charge for delivering one pallet was a massive €79! She then called Castorama – they charge a mere €160 for delivery, per order. Even if you're only buying a bathplug.

The small company in Aubigny called Weldom offers delivery for €30, so it looks like we'll be buying stuff from them. This also explains why so many people here have car trailers. It's our intention to get one of these as well, but the car will need to be re-registered in France first (because we'll need a number plate for the trailer). This process is in hand but like anything here, it takes time. We were originally intending to get four 1000-litre water containers for a rainwater recovery system; these turn out to be too expensive so we'll get six 500-litre barrels instead. There is a suitable space for these at the rear of the barn.

In between showers of rain we managed to plough up the vegetable garden using the motor-driven tiller. It was the first time LSS and I had used one of these machines but after a while we got the hang of it. The first project is finally under way! Two hours later, we were rewarded by the sight of a large expanse of turned-over soil. It will need to be done a couple more times before we're ready to plant anything though.

Following our dusty labours, we carried the bathtub into the kitchen and had a well-deserved bath next to the warmth of the wood stove.

Saturday 21st

Rain, rain, rain. It's rained every day this week and the ditches are overflowing. Still, at least the pond is filling up. In between showers we fed the carp with stale bread. There are some nice-sized fish in the pond – some over 40cm long.

LSS tackled the water tank ("*ballon*") and managed to get water to appear at the kitchen tap. It's pale brown in colour (the water, not the tap) possibly due to rust in the pipes. But it's wet, and at least we'll be able to wash the walls and floors with it.

I should perhaps explain about this *ballon* thing. It's the French term for a pressurized tank. There is a well at the property, which has been the sole source of household water since the house was built in eighteen hundred and something. By the simple expedient of tying a large washer to a piece of rope, and lowering it into the well, I have determined that it is just over four metres deep, and the water depth is three metres. A pipe runs through a hole in the brickwork about half-way down the well and disappears down into the water. The other end of this pipe runs underground to one of the outbuildings, where it terminates at an ancient three-phase electric pump. From this pump, a short length of leaky bandaged pipe runs above a collection of jam-jars (to collect the drips) into the galvanised steel tank which is supposedly able to withstand a pressure of 10 bars. The pump is connected electrically via an ancient three-phase pressure switch, which the aged FIL had simply wired up to a single phase plug somehow connected to a three-phase supply. The idea is that when the pump is switched on, water fills up this tank, and once the pressure inside reaches around 3 bars, the pump switches off.

However, up until today we have not been able to get any water to enter the tank at all when the pump was switched on. Examining the setup, LSS discovered a small bolt on the pump inlet, and after some head-scratching we worked out that this must be the inlet used for priming the pump. Pouring two litres of water into the hole with the aid of a funnel meant the pump was finally operational.

Whilst LSS was busying herself in supplying the household with rusty water, I finished working on the fruit trees in the orchard, pruning off the dead branches. LSS then assisted me with removing the remaining brambles. I have never known plants to have such long, persistent roots!

All this time, the wood stove was burning quietly away in the kitchen, and as LSS had had the brilliant idea of sticking some foil-wrapped potatoes into the oven side of it first thing this morning, we now have some roast potatoes for dinner.

Speaking of wood stoves, as I mentioned soon after we arrived, one of the first things we had to do was to empty the house and barn of junk. One of the things in the barn was an old horse-drawn cart which was covered with bits of wood and fruit boxes. We later managed to sell the cart (for next to nothing, which was probably a fair representation of its value) through a French website, to someone who wanted it for his front garden as an ornament.

But the woodworm/termites had been busy; not only the cart, but the majority of the wood pieces were infested. Mould was in evidence too. The wood scrap simply had to go. But instead of just throwing it away, we decided to extract whatever remained of the calories of energy it contained by burning it in the kitchen stove.

Of course if we had told anyone (especially the aged FIL) what we were doing, there would have been gasps of horror. "You can't burn that in the kitchen stove! It won't burn well! You'll block the chimney! Go and cut down a nice tree instead!" Well, chimneys can be cleaned, *n'est ce pas?* The way I look at it is that we have wood to burn which would otherwise just be thrown away. I reflected for a moment on a documentary about Ethiopia we saw on British television a while back. The camera crew followed one young woman who lived in a tent made of animal skins. Her earthly riches consisted of the tent, a cooking pot, and a goat. Her husband was off somewhere patrolling the border with his AK-47. Of course the area around her tent, for as far as the eye could see, was bare. Not a tree or a blade of grass in sight. So when it came to deciding whether to burn our wood in the kitchen stove, I pictured this woman wandering along with her goat and seeing something on the ground. "Ooh, a twig! I can heat my house for a week with that! And cook a goat." Riches are relative.

Yes, we did have to have the chimney cleaned. But then again, we don't know when this was done last, so we can't blame the poor quality wood for that!

The fruit boxes have been stacked in one of the outbuildings which will see later use as a chicken coop. If we can't use the fruit boxes for anything else I'm sure they'll come in handy for lighting fires.

As far as furniture was concerned, there were two large cupboards in the house. These had not been moved, dusted, or otherwise touched for about thirty years either. Of course the woodworm and/or termites had had a field day here too. The first cupboard simply fell apart when we tried to move it. This, too, ended up becoming a pile of wood ash at the bottom of the garden. The other cupboard was in slightly better condition, because only the doors fell off. I did consider using this cupboard in the workshop for tool storage but decided my tools would be better off without it. I suspect it will suffer the same fate as the first.

Today also saw the final family dinner at the aged FIL's house. Up until this point, we had been going there to eat with him (when the aged FIL wasn't in hospital, that is). Well, we took along the baked potatoes we'd cooked in the wood stove, intending to have these with a Bolognese-type sauce which LSS whipped up. Very nice they were too. Except the aged FIL didn't like them.

"I DON'T EAT POTATOES WITH THEIR SKINS ON!" he complained loudly. "Fine, cook your own supper then," LSS retorted. He decided to go to bed, even though we hadn't finished eating, and banged his wheelchair into my chair on his way past.

From now on we'll have our supper at our own house once LSS has fed the aged FIL and put him to bed.

Sunday 22nd

The cousin of LSS, a farmer chappy whom I shall call JP (because those are his initials), turned up with his wife to say hello. During the conversation about how we were getting on and what we were going to do next, we happened to mention we didn't think much of the French way of storing cold water, which is by means of a pressurised tank.

The setup we inherited means that when you want to turn the tap on, you need to go and switch the pump on in order to fill the tank. This then works fine for up to 24 hours but over that time period the pressure leaks out of the tank – so no further water comes from the tap. You then need to go into the outbuilding to switch the pump on again.

"*Mais non!*" says JP. "That's not the way it should work. You see, it's completely automatic. The water pressure drops, the pump switches itself on, pumps the water up from the well, and fills the container. The pressure rises, the pump switches itself off, and *voilà*, you have constant water."

LSS and I looked at each other blankly. This was definitely not the case with our setup.

"Ah, look, I'll show you. You've probably not switched it on correctly," he said. So we all trot out to the shed where he gets his first view of the tank.

"Hmm. You have a leakage of air here. You need to undo this tube and re-tighten it. Do you have a spanner?"

I pointed wordlessly at a pair of the aged FIL's aged adjustable spanners which were laying on top of the aged tank - presumably left there for just this sort of eventuality. Personally I hadn't liked the look of these spanners, as they didn't appear to be good for anything. Unless you needed a couple of paperweights. And didn't mind rust-marks on your paper.

"*Ah, bon.*" he said. He struggled with the aforementioned bits of metal (I hesitate to call them tools) for a few minutes. Finally:

"What is this *connerie*? Don't you have any decent spanners?"

I fetched my Bahco lifetime-warranty adjustable wrench. Which, unsurprisingly, did a much better job of undoing the nuts. Having satisfied himself that he had solved the leakage of air, he pressed the "On" button. And was rewarded with... absolutely nothing.

"*Merde.* Why isn't this switch working? Oh, I see, you'll need to drain the tank first."

We connected a hosepipe to the bottom tap and drained the entire 200 litres of water into the garden. He then switched the pump on. The tank filled. And kept filling. And the pump kept running. Pressurised water started to leak from sundry connections. At this point the group of interested spectators - namely LSS, JP's wife, and myself, retired hurriedly outside, where we watched wide-eyed through the open doorway.

"*Ah, c'est le bordel!*" He unscrewed the pressure gauge, and was immediately soaked with a deluge of rusty water. Hurriedly, he switched the pump off, and then proceeded to dismantle and rewire the electrical connections on the pressure switch.

"*Bon!*" With this grunt of satisfaction, he switched on. The mains electricity supply tripped.

Having rewired the switch for the third time, with another interim tripping of the mains electricity supply, the pump again groaned into life. However, no water was entering the tank, because of course, by this time, all the water in the pipes had drained back into the well. We had to pour two bottles of water into the pump in order to prime it again.

"*Merde.* It shouldn't be doing that," he exclaimed. No, really? You don't say.

Finally the tank was filled. Then drained. Then filled.

Finally admitting defeat, he said that he had the feeling that the pressure switch was faulty and should be replaced.

So two hours of labour later we were back where we started. With a manually-operated, non-pressure-retaining, water tank. However, instead of being a very pale orange colour, the water is now dark brown with all the rust which has been stirred up from the frequent emptying and refilling.

"Remind me not to ask him to fix anything else for us," I said to LSS as they drove off. "And isn't it funny that generally the first words you remember in a foreign language are the naughty ones?"

<u>Monday 23rd</u>

We've been here a month! And it's still raining. And cold. I had to check the local paper just to make sure we hadn't suddenly been transported to Ireland. Nope, it was still France. (Apologies to any Irish reading this, I'm sure it's not always raining there). Actually the locals, when discovering that we've lived in Britain previously, are always sympathetic. "Oh you poor things. It rains all the time there." They just smile disbelievingly when we tell them we have found it to be wetter here.

Despite the rain, we managed to have a bath by our now accustomed procedure of carrying the bathtub into the kitchen again and heating the water in large saucepans on the wood stove. The bathwater is a bit browner than usual, thanks to JP's efforts yesterday. Still, at least we're now clean. We'll never again take a tiled bathroom for granted.

An Orange/France Telecom engineer telephoned us today regarding the problem we'd reported with the internet.

"Eh? We haven't reported any problem with the internet."

"Oh? Well, it says here you've reported that you're not getting a two mega connection, only one mega, so we'll need to arrange for an engineer's visit."

"Ohhhhhhhh, I see. No, look, we didn't report it. The other engineer reported it. We didn't know it was a problem. In fact it isn't a problem. We're very pleased with the slowness. It works. We don't want you touching it, we're quite happy, please leave us alone, we don't need any other engineers, and I want my mummy."

The doctor visited the aged FIL today, and recommended that he gets a '*lit médicalisé*' (a medical bed, the type you find in hospitals), to facilitate the nurse giving him a bed-bath (when we are finally able to actually find a nurse that does this, that is). In order to get a bed, a prescription is needed. Unfortunately, this doctor was a locum, as the usual doctor is on holiday, and he forgot to fill out the prescription form. So LSS called the surgery, where she spoke to the receptionist-secretary-administrator.

"We need a prescription to get a medical bed, a '*lit médicalisé*'," she stated.

"This prescription, is it a renewal?"

"?!"

I told her she should have said, "Yes, he's finished eating the old one."

Wildlife diary: We've discovered that there is a duck nesting in the reeds next to the pond. I only noticed the nest because I happened to walk up to the pond, and the female flew noisily out of the reeds. There appear to be seven eggs in

the nest, all a pale duck-egg blue (obviously). I beat a hasty
retreat as I don't want them abandoned.

Tuesday 24th

After visiting the HSBC in Brinon and filling in even more
forms, my French bank account is finally opened! Of course I
can't actually use it yet, as I don't have a card or chequebook;
but it's a start.

On the way back from Brinon, LSS suddenly said, "Look,
dear."

"Yes dear?" I replied.

"No, dear," she said.

"What ARE you on about?" I asked.

"Deer! *Chevreuil.* Things with four legs in that field we
just passed."

"Ohhhhhhhhh...."

Unfortunately the aged FIL proved to be particularly incon-
tinent today, with the consequence that not only his pyjamas,
but all the bedclothes, including blankets, needed to be – shall
we just say – thoroughly washed.

In the evening the very first carer turned up to give him
his supper and take him to the lavatory (which unsurprisingly
he didn't need).

Wildlife diary: I'm pleased to report the duck has
not taken my unexpected visit to heart, and is still on
the nest.

Wednesday 25th

Our letter box is finally installed! We can receive post!
Hooray! Ooh, a bill. Not hooray.

Yet more rain. We went to Leroy Merlin in St. Doulchard in order to get some materials to finally start the renovations. Before getting a shopping trolley, we thought we would look around first to see if they had what we wanted. It took us a while to locate things, but in the end we found that they stocked most of what we were looking for. However, as it was getting close to lunchtime we didn't actually buy anything. Not only do shops close over lunchtime here (so we would not have had time to fill the shopping trolley with everything we'd found), but we had to get back to the aged FIL to give him his lunch and take him to the lavatory. Instead, we thought we'd just order everything we needed over the Internet and have it delivered, despite the high delivery fees. It later turned out this was a big mistake; we should have made the aged FIL wait and bought the things we needed. Especially as he was being difficult as usual and didn't want to eat. He's finally realised we're not eating with him any more.

Wildlife diary: On the way back from town, we'd slowed to walking pace in order to turn into the side road leading to our house, when we saw a very unusual sight; a Reeves' pheasant. These are fairly rare birds; according to Wikipedia there are only 2 000 birds remaining in the wild. It obviously resented the large green-coloured object invading its territory, because it displayed aggressively towards the car, standing on tiptoes and flapping its wings madly. Just to annoy it, I drove forward slowly. It was completely undeterred. "This is my patch, and I'm not giving way to you, no matter how big you are!" We watched its display for a few minutes and then left it in peace.

Thursday 26th

The brambles have been having a field day near the pond, so today was Bramble Nemesis Day. It's been a nightmare getting rid of the roots - some of them are over three metres long. I also successfully trimmed a couple of large tree branches which were overhanging the pond.

I also bought myself a new watch on Amazon.fr (a cheap and cheerful €14.99 Casio) because I don't want to risk ruining my non-€14.99 Seiko. I also successfully ordered some pet food tin lids from Ebay, so am once again live in the internet shopping mall. However, neither LSS nor I have received our French chequebooks or cards yet.

We had some turkey stew for dinner tonight, compliments of the kitchen wood stove. This afternoon we also visited the aged aunt to once again beg the use of her shower.

Wildlife diary: Heard a cuckoo for the first time today. It sounded just like the clock!

Friday 27th

Following our abortive visit to Leroy Merlin (whose website was not exactly user-friendly either) we decided to visit the next DIY place on our list, called Weldom. The closest branch is in Aubigny, about thirty km away. We are determined to spend some money, and took a long time compiling a shopping list. This contains items like six 500-litre barrels for rainwater recovery; guttering, and hydraulic lime for re-plastering the interior walls. Yes, I know you can use non-hydraulic lime, but hydraulic lime is better for damp conditions. And I wouldn't say the interior walls were exactly wet, but put it this way – if you hung wallpaper, it would all be on the floor the following morning.

Anyway, I digress. As I mentioned, we had discovered that trying to order DIY stuff in France is a nightmare compared to the UK. In Britain, simply pop in to a company like Screwfix, and say, "I'll have that, and that, and that, and deliver it" and they say "Certainly, you'll have it tomorrow." Or you can simply buy it online.

So, with naïve hopes of a similar reception, we arrived at Weldom, and asked for assistance. We were handed over to a youth in his early twenties.

"We want this, this, that and that. Oh yes, and a box of these."

"*Non,*" was the reply.

"What do you mean '*Non*'? We want to give you lots of money."

"*Ah, non,*" he repeated. "We don't do things that way here. We first of all need to photocopy your shopping list, which will take twenty minutes. Then we return and give you your list back, take your address and phone number and email address."

"Fine, so when do we get our stuff then?" (You understand I'm translating here. I took no part in the conversation as LSS was doing the talking. Well she *is* French).

"We'll email you this afternoon with a quote."

"But we don't need a quote. We want to pay for everything now!" LSS exclaimed.

"*Mais, non!* First we send you the quote. Then you sign the quote saying everything is *Bon pour accord*, and fax it

51

to this number. Then you send us a cheque. Then when the cheque has cleared, a week later we deliver. *Bon?*"

No, mate, not *bon* at all.

They did indeed email us a quote late in the afternoon. Unfortunately some items had been omitted, and wrong items added, so LSS emailed them back asking for corrections.

Wildlife diary: On the way back from Aubigny I saw my first wild boar! It was running alongside a field of rape, with its tail in the air just like a warthog. The duck is still in residence in the pond.

Saturday 28th

LSS tackled the remaining brambles around the pond, and we've put them into a large pile ready for burning as soon as the weather improves. We can now clearly see the pond from the kitchen window instead of seeing a jungle of waving spiky tangled foliage. Some of the bramble roots will still need to be dug out but that's a job for another day.

I cut some more bits of woodworm for the wood stove, and then we paid a visit to a local fair called *"Musicalies"*. If you're keen on ancient French folk music complete with odd-shaped instruments, this is the fair for you. We were more bemused than anything else.

Unexpectedly, a carer turned up to feed and water the aged FIL, and they brought a schedule of visits for the following week, so it looks like LSS will have some much-needed respite from looking after a cantankerous parent.

Wildlife diary: Heard the cuckoo. It sounds like there are two of them now, calling to each other slightly out of synch.

Sunday 29th

LSS spent two hours looking after the aged FIL this morning. When we arrived, the aged FIL was jumping up and down (well, as much as a person in bed can jump up and down) because his electric heaters had stopped working. I thought it was probably because he's running three electric heaters via two different extension leads from a ten-ampere light socket in the kitchen. We have previously expressed surprise that the house hasn't burnt down.

I checked the fuses and found that everything was in order. These are the very old-style ceramic fuses which were quite difficult to extract from their sockets; more so because they probably haven't been touched for decades. I would also be quite surprised if the fuse wire itself was actually fuse wire. It could quite possibly be a length of ordinary fencing wire, as it looked a lot stronger than fuse wire should. The whole house really needs re-wiring, but the aged FIL refuses to do this because he says he does not have any money.

This is also the reason he doesn't have central heating. Or a bathroom. Or hot water. Or an inside lavatory. Or...

As to the reason why he's in bed all the time, it's nothing physical. It seems to be a psychological block; he is simply too afraid of falling over. The doctor is of the opinion that he'll never be able to walk unaided again. And he absolutely refuses to use a walker (one of those four-legged contraptions like a small stepladder) even though he's been given one. At that moment, JP (remember the water tank repair?) arrived with his son for a visit. As they live in a similar type of farmhouse, the two of them disappeared into the attic by way of an external wooden ladder. (I call it an attic - actually it's the second floor of the house, but it's just a vast empty space which was originally used for storing straw and other animal feed.) They discovered a junction box which had a loose connection, and the aged FIL was happy again as his electric heaters were once more glowing nicely.

As it's Sunday, we didn't do very much (well we do need one day a week off!) apart from having a bath, which is a job in itself. Once again it was too cold and grey outside, so we carried the bath into the kitchen next to the woodstove and filled it with water heated on the aforementioned kitchen appliance. Later the skies cleared and we had our first glimpse of sunshine for absolutely ages.

It's very frustrating not to be able to get on with renovating the house, but we can't do anything until we have the materials! Hopefully next week will see some progress on this front, although with all the bank holidays in France at this time of year, it is probably unlikely.

Wildlife diary: Heard the cuckoos again in the late afternoon, calling to each other from the chestnut trees opposite the house.

Monday 30th

LSS tackled the garden with the tiller again whilst I got on with cutting more bits of wood with the chainsaw for the hungry kitchen wood-burner. LSS had just managed to get all the soil turned over before the rain started again. It looks like our pile of brambles will not be ready to burn for some time yet!

In the post we received a reply from Honda France regarding the *Certificate de Conformité*. They've sent us a pile of forms which need to be filled in by an official dealership, so we've booked the bike in to visit the closest dealership in Blois this Friday. They also mentioned that once the forms had been filled in, they would need to be sent back to Honda France together with a cheque for €140.

LSS received a reply from Hyundai as well. They don't need the vehicle to be inspected first, but they do want a cheque for €200 for the Certificate. They'll have to wait until our chequebooks have been received!

Even though re-registering the vehicles in France is going to cost some money, we've calculated that this is still a cheaper option than selling them for next to nothing in the UK and buying replacements here. Second-hand vehicles in France are a great deal more expensive than they are in Britain. In fact we know several people who have made a trip to the UK for just that purpose.

There was still no news from Weldom, so in the afternoon LSS called them.

"I've emailed you a quote to be corrected."

"Oh, quotes? Very sorry, the staff member who deals with quotes is on holiday. Call again on Wednesday."

Isn't French customer service wonderful?

Wildlife diary: Unfortunately there's bad news. Some sort of predator found the duck's nest, and left a neat pile of eggshells. No wonder we haven't seen the ducks recently.

May

I T is finally warm enough to start planting in the garden,
and we become bored with plum jam. We visit the lady
with the moustache, and undertake a battle with Colorado
Beetles.

Tuesday 1st

When I was small, and Christmas trees were tall... the first
of May always reminds me of the Bee Gees. Don't ask me
why, but time has passed us by.

This morning we paid yet another visit to the aged aunt
of LSS to collect our redirected mail and have a much-needed
shower. This time we came prepared, with a bottle of vinegar
and some caustic soda. The shower head went into a small
bowl filled with vinegar, where it stayed whilst we all had
some coffee. Some of the caustic soda was sprinkled down the
shower drain where it did a sterling job at increasing the rate
of drainage. Now one can have a shower without having to
jump around to get wet, and without the shower tray filling
up with water. Well, the aged aunt is over eighty, so at least
there was something we could do for her!

Wildlife diary: Three pheasant (a cock bird with two
hens in tow), a roe deer, and a surprise! I happened to
glance out of the kitchen window beyond the pond, and
saw what I thought was a dog lying in the long grass. The
swift application of the 10x50 binoculars which are now kept
handily on the kitchen table revealed that it was in fact
a young fox.

A few minutes later it was joined by another youngster, and then Mum arrived. They obviously have television in their den tuned to the BBC's Wildlife channel, because David Attenborough recently did a documentary on the polar bear. Bear (ha – a pun!) with me a moment and I'll explain. One of the articles in the documentary described and showed the polar bear hunting seals, and bouncing heavily on the ice to break into the seal's lair. Well, this is what one of the fox-cubs was doing. I didn't see any seals, but I'm sure he thought they were there. The two cubs then chased each other up and down for a while until their mother was ready to take them off hunting.

Strangely enough this entire episode was also watched by the pheasants, which were standing still in amazement. The cuckoos are still calling to each other.

Wednesday 2nd

Wildlife diary: I'll start today's entry with this, just to get it out of the way. We saw a roe deer. And the three pheasant. Again. And the two cuckoos are still calling. Throughout the day. Constantly.

Today was yet another frustrating day as far as doing any DIY was concerned. LSS telephoned Weldom again to check the status of our quote. Unfortunately the only member of staff that deals with quotes had gone home, because they only work mornings. It would have been nice to have been told this by the last person LSS spoke to. (Chorus: "You didn't ask.")

I suppose it's all thanks to the 35-hour work week which France enjoys. So there's still no progress on the getting-the-house-liveable front. We'll have to phone again tomorrow.

The good news is that the cat seems to have lost the two ticks she picked up last week. We noticed them on Saturday, and having unfortunately been a bit slack in the anti-tick and anti-flea regime for the past month, we had to take drastic action and put some of that spot-on stuff on the back of her neck. This time she didn't go into a scratching frenzy like she did the first time we used it, so maybe she's getting used to having Fipronil coursing through her system. It also stands to reason that today was the day they decided to die and drop off, because this morning we bought a tick-remover tweezers-thingy from the chemist. Oh well, we'll be ready for the next lot.

Even buying a new chainsaw guide bar has been fraught with difficulties. The local chainsaw-and-general-agricultural-equipment shop didn't have the right size in stock and told me I would have to order it. I didn't. Back home, I managed to find one online from a shop in Alsace, at two-thirds of the price I was quoted locally - even including postage.

Speaking of postage, today's post consisted of a letter from HSBC telling me my pin for the new card which they had now received, and saying I could now collect my card in the local branch.

French official correspondence is amazing; it does not seem to have evolved since the nineteenth century! The letter concluded:

"We pray you agree, Madam, Sir, with the expression of our distinguished sentiments." I think even Charles Dickens would have said "Huh?"

(For the purists out there, here's the actual wording: *"Nous vous prions d'agréer, Madame, Monsieur, l'expression de nos sentiments distingués."*)

I also ordered some ecological fly-traps online, from Ebay this time. Well, that's another thing you can't buy locally. I've noticed that now that the weather has started to warm up, there are more and more of the little blighters around. And having visited this place several times in summers past, I know what it can be like. The thing is, although we're not inundated yet, they do breed like, er, flies.

This afternoon, as it had finally stopped raining, we tried lighting the pile of brambles in the garden. We'd been eyeing this with anticipation for several days, waiting to get our revenge. Unfortunately we discovered that the pile was still too wet to burn, so we'll need to wait a bit longer.

In the evening we finished our dinner of turkey leg stew, reheated on the kitchen range. It's a cantankerous old thing, a *Rosiere* by name. (The range, not the turkey leg stew). According to the chimney sweep, "They go on for ever!" Oh no they don't, mate, because the aged FIL's gave up the ghost just before winter, and it was a more modern one than this old thing. He has had electric heaters going in every room all winter, and we're all waiting with bated breath for the electricity bill. We're taking bets on it being bigger than the Greek national deficit.

After dinner, LSS asked "Would you like an apple?"

"Yes please", I replied.

It was a good job she looked twice before handing it to me, as it happened to be a turnip.

Thursday 3rd

Sunshine at last! Lots of lovely sunshine.

The morning didn't start too well. LSS called Weldom again and was put through to several different people, none of whom had any knowledge of the quote we'd requested. Finally she managed to speak to the original youth who took our order, and whilst on the phone to him she received the quote by email. Obviously he'd forgotten to hit the "send" button last week and had hurriedly remedied this oversight.

We checked the quote and were pleasantly surprised that everything appeared correct. Now for the next challenge; paying for it!

LSS called Weldom back and spoke to the youth again, offering to give card details over the phone so that the order could be placed.

"Ah, non!" Quel horreur! "You want to do what? Pay for it over the phone? *Non*, we can't do things like that here. It's not possible. You need to send us a cheque."

At this point LSS lost patience. To cut a long story short, we're going to have to go to Aubigny tomorrow to physically put the card in the card reader in order to pay for the goods. The good news is that the manager will be there tomorrow, so we are going to have STERN WORDS with him and demand a discount.

We were then surprised by the arrival of JP and son; they had dropped in to visit the aged FIL and he had (once again) complained that his heaters had stopped working. As they couldn't find the key to his outside "office" containing the electricity mains switch, they came to ask where it was. It turned out it was in the usual drawer in the kitchen, but they had missed it.

A further visit to the upstairs space revealed yet another junction box with a loose connection. I stayed well out of the way, and instead dug around in the tool shed to see if I could find a chainsaw sharpening guide. (This is a metal bar which enables you to file down the anti-kickback depth gauges to the correct height). I managed to find one, but it's for a different sized chain. Sigh. I think another Internet order is required.

We then drove to Brinon so I could collect my new bank card and chequebook. I was able to use the card, but still can't check my account online as I'm waiting for the login details. As we were in Brinon, which is where the aged FIL's doctor is located, LSS took the opportunity to drop in to renew one of the aged FIL's prescriptions and have a chat about his condition. The outcome was positive; the doctor said that the aged FIL should not really be living in his current conditions but should instead be in a retirement home where he could have proper care. So that particular branch of paperwork is the next thing we'll need to tackle. I expect the aged FIL will need to sign something though, so I doubt anything will come of it. "I was born in this house, and I'll die in it!" he has said, more than once.

Because my Pan European ST1100 is booked in to the Honda dealership in Blois tomorrow for an examination to determine whether it is a legal vehicle for French roads, I wheeled it out of the barn this afternoon to check that it was ready for the trip. I discovered that the back tyre was flat, as I'd managed to pick up a screw in the tread. It must have been on the trip down because the head of the screw was shiny with wear. Fortunately I always carry a tyre plugger on the bike so I soon had the puncture repaired. The bike was extremely dusty as well; it's been parked in the barn for a month! We managed to find our hosepipe reel, but then had an entertaining twenty minutes looking for the plastic connector which connects the pipe to an ordinary tap thread. Eventually we found it, connected the hosepipe to the *ballon* (the one which you have to switch on the pump every five minutes to refill it) and gave the bike a wash. Once I'd finished, LSS decided to wash all the mud off her car as well. The roads leading to the property are farm tracks, and with all the rain we've had they've become quagmires. I'm pleased to report the sides of the car are now once again green instead of mud-brown.

Although our garden is not yet ready to provide us with any food, we're not short of anything to drink. And no, we haven't had to buy any booze since we've been here. The late MIL was a compulsive shopper (there is a name for this disease but it escapes me at the moment). Anyway, we discovered some wooden boxes in a disused outbuilding at the aged FIL's property. They contained bottles of white wine and rosé, all at 1997 bargain-basement prices, and all with the distinct possibility that they had become bottles of vinegar.

The late MIL hardly ever drank wine; and the aged FIL has said if she bought it, it won't be any good, so he doesn't want any.

So, you understand, for health and safety reasons we need

to ascertain whether these fifteen-year old supermarket bottles of plonk have turned into vinegar or not.

So far, not.

Wildlife diary: those blasted cuckoos are starting to get on our nerves. We're hoping the cat will sort them out but no luck so far.

Friday 4th

At last, there's been some progress. Not without some minor mishaps; but progress nonetheless. The day started as usual; raining. Still, we had to be at the Honda dealership in Blois at 9:00 a.m. so by 8:00 a.m. we were suitably dressed and on the bike, ready to go.

Unfortunately we only covered about fifty metres before the mishap. In order to get to a tarmac road, we have some 400 metres of farm track to negotiate. Although this is a public road (and thus presumably maintained by the public purse), it's not much used; with the result that it's covered with grass.

Rain + soil + grass = very slippery surface.

Rain + soil + grass + motorcycle = motorcycle lying on its side on the grass.

Now lifting a nearly 300-kilogram motorcycle from the horizontal position to the vertical requires a special technique, which involves planting your bum in the middle of the seat and using your leg muscles to right the motorcycle. I've done this before successfully, but never on grass. Unfortunately grass does not provide a decent surface for the grip of motorcycle boots, so I was forced to use more back muscle than leg muscle. So as a result, this was written whilst sitting precariously upright on a hard chair, as sitting in any other position was painful.

Anyway, with the motorcycle the right way up again, we proceeded slipperily (that's not a word but it should be) along the grassy track at less than walking pace until we finally reached the tarmac surface. The tyres felt as though they didn't have much grip for the first few kilometres until the mud had worked its way out of the treads, so we proceeded at a very sedate rate until I felt the response of the bike was more like its usual self. Once we got to the Honda dealer, we handed over all the paperwork which Honda France had sent us, and the bike was taken through to the workshop area.

Now, I may have mentioned this once or twice, but the bike is a Honda. And Honda France is... er... Honda. So their company actually manufactured the thing.

But they had requested all sorts of details; make and model of the spark plugs and ignition leads, type and size of tyres, exhaust part numbers, headlight part numbers, indicator part numbers, stop light part numbers..... the list went on and on – I kid you not. An hour or so later, the mechanic returned and held a whispered conversation with the staff member behind the counter. They then both disappeared into the workshop for a while. Some time elapsed before the staff member returned, to say there was a problem.

"Look," he said. "If I write down all the part numbers like they're asking, you simply won't get a *Certificate de Conformité* at all. Because, for example, you've got Avon tyres fitted. They're not the make specified by Honda, which is Bridgestone. You don't have Honda exhausts; you have custom-made stainless steel ones. Which I can quite imagine will last a lot longer than the ones fitted by Honda, but are not the type that Honda specifies. So, as we happen to have a standard ST1100 in the workshop, what I've done is taken the part numbers from that and written that on the list. However, you will need to have the headlight changed. Although the beam of yours is not deflected to the left but a straight-ahead type, the French requirements are that the beam is deflected to the right."

Suitably grateful, we made another appointment for next Friday to have the work done. Now a simple thing like changing a headlight I could of course do myself. I had happened to mention this.

"Oh no you can't," he exclaimed in horror. "You see, the vehicle licensing authority require a different piece of paper stating that the work has been done in an approved dealership, with an official dealership stamp to prove it."

The trip back home was much more enjoyable; although it was still raining at times. Once we got back to the grassy track though, I made LSS get off and walk for the last fifty metres. The added weight at the rear would probably have provided more grip, but I thought I'd try negotiating the tricky section without a passenger. This was fortunately carried out without any further incident.

After putting the bike away and having a peaceful lunch, we took the car to Aubigny to visit Weldom. Again.

This time, the manager was in, and greeted our request for a discount with the customary intake of breath through pursed lips. However, after some inconsequential chatting about how bad things were in France and the state of the world in general, he mellowed a bit, and the result was that not only were we able to actually pay for our order, we got a discount which was the equivalent of having free delivery, and everything has been promised for Monday 14th. We may finally be able to get some work done!

No wildlife diary today, simply because we weren't here most of the time!

Saturday 5th

I bought a soil testing kit a few weeks ago from Amazon, and on Thursday last week finally got around to taking a couple of samples from the garden. At least we'll be able to determine whether the soil is acidic or not, and how much more rabbit poo is required. Unfortunately the weather was not letting the soil samples dry properly, so yesterday evening I put them in the oven to finish drying. Tomorrow I'll have a look at the pH reading.

This morning we fetched a parcel from the Post Office – it was my chainsaw chain sharpening machine! One can sharpen a chainsaw chain by hand; but it's fiddly. One also has to make sure each cutter is given the exact same number of strokes with the file. A sharpening machine can do a more accurate job, but the danger is that one can easily remove too much metal. Yesterday after we returned from Weldom I filed the depth gauges down a bit – they were still in factory-supplied condition despite the fact that the aged FIL had sharpened the chain cutters to less than half their original length. For the uninitiated, when you sharpen the chain of a chainsaw, not only do you need to file the cutters to leave a nice sharp edge, but you also need to check the height of the anti-kickback depth gauges – if you don't do this, your chain can be as sharp as you like but it won't cut butter. I'm pleased to report that it now cuts through wood with great rapidity, leading to less wear and tear on both saw and operator!

Unfortunately at three p.m. the heavens opened again, putting the kybosh on our plans to have a barbecue tonight. However, we always have a Plan B, and LSS had fired up the wood stove in order to make one of her special dishes, a corned beef pie. At around four p.m. I suddenly remembered it was our wedding anniversary. Fortunately LSS had forgotten this as well, so I wasn't in trouble. Seven years as a married couple, and fourteen years together in total – my, doesn't time fly!

Wildlife diary: zero sightings of anything due to the rain, but I did notice that some rabbits had been digging holes in the field opposite the house.

Sunday 6th

This morning LSS visited the aged FIL again. He's now being looked after three times a day, which has eased the burden on us tremendously. She managed to get him to walk from the bed to the kitchen; a distance of about five metres. Still, I suppose it's progress.

Two days ago he decided that his diet should consist mainly of prunes, so unfortunately one of the carers has had to deal with the inevitable result.

I analysed the soil from the garden and was fairly pleased to discover that the pH was 6.5 - slightly acidic, but nothing too serious. In fact potatoes prefer a slightly more acidic soil, so we'll see how they do. Potassium levels are low, and so is the nitrogen level, so I think we need to dig a lot more rabbit poo into the garden, as well as planting some of the Leguminosae family (beans and peas - these add nitrogen to the soil). Phosphorous levels are off the chart though, probably due to the aged FIL's penchant for buying superphosphate in large quantities. See, that's the thing I don't understand. The farmers/smallholders of a certain generation planted vegetable gardens in profusion. But they were told that in order to get decent crops, they needed to buy lots of chemical products from the agricultural suppliers. If you added up the cost of all this stuff, and included the labour, it would actually have been cheaper for them to have bought all their vegetables from the supermarket in the first place!

Due to the rain this afternoon, we once again had a bath in the kitchen. So much for having a barbecue tonight.

We took advantage of a lull in between rain showers to examine a couple of large wooden barrels, which were originally used for storing cider many, many years ago. I removed one end of each of them by the simple method of tapping the wood gently with an axe, and we rolled them closer to the pond where they will probably fill up with rainwater in a very short time. The idea is that one of them will be used by LSS to brew a concoction of nettle soup (not for consumption, but as an insecticide/fertilizer for the garden). The other barrel could possibly be used for holding any carp we catch once the weather has improved enough to go fishing. (I'm not that keen on eating carp straight from the pond as they taste somewhat muddy; hopefully if we put a freshly-caught fish into a barrel of clean rainwater for a few days this will help to get rid of the muddy taste. I think it's worth a try.)

Wildlife diary: The frogs are now out in force around the pond. Not much big game was around today. I have noticed that when the sun is shining, the lizards frolic up and down the south-facing walls of the house. Most of them are tail-less, having no doubt had a close encounter with the cat.

Monday 7th

So, France has a new President. Thank goodness we don't have the TV connected. But the euro has decreased in value against the sterling, which is good news as far as we're concerned. In today's post we received our second quote for connecting us to the village water supply which terminates some 400 metres away. The first quote was just under €10 000. This one? A few cents under €20 000! It looks like we'll be getting a borehole instead. One of the advantages of having our own borehole will be the lack of a monthly water bill!

Oh yes, and the fly traps arrived in the post box too. These are basically small plastic buckets in which you put some tasty (for flies that is) liquid bait, and then hang them up outside. Apparently it takes 48 hours before they start to take effect. Well, LSS had cooked some very old pasta which we were going to feed to the fish, and had left it outside to cool. About thirty seconds later, some twenty-odd flies had immediately drowned themselves in the hot liquid in the saucepan, so I'm starting to think we should have used the pasta as bait in the fly-traps instead.

The sun appeared today for the first time in ages, so we were able to have our long-overdue barbecue this evening.

However, even though the meat had been marinating for two days in readiness, it was still unbelievably tough! It was tasty enough, but we won't be buying that particular cut of beef ribs again. Well yes, all right, it was at a reduced price. Now we know why.

Still, the toughness of the meat was alleviated by having three bottles of Martin's Wallop between us. (This is the brand name of our home-brewed beer, which weighs in at a respectable 6.3% ABV). This is a record, as the two of us normally only drink two bottles. It must be the air here. Well, that's my excuse.

LSS took advantage of the sunshine by driving the tiller through the garden again this afternoon; the soil should just about be ready to receive the first seedlings/seeds. I think radishes and lettuces will be the first plant life to experience our pH-tested, rabbit-poo enriched soil.

With the trials and tribulations we've experienced with the aged FIL recently, LSS was starting to wonder whether we'd done the right thing in moving to France, thinking that she would have been better off staying with the small company for which she was working (she was the Sales Office Manager). Well, she received an email from one of the remaining staff there, saying the company would soon be closing its Reading office completely, making the staff there redundant, and moving oop North to Lincolnshire. So at least that took care of any remaining doubts she had!

Wildlife diary: On the way back from visiting the aged FIL, we saw a coypu. It leaped out of the water-filled ditch and ran for cover, then changed its mind, stopped, and stared at the car. It's also known as a nutria, and its local name is *ragondin*. This herbivore was introduced to Europe for its fur, but is quite destructive as far as the local habitat is concerned. It's also edible - see photograph on back cover.

Other than that, I've noticed that the rabbits have now started excavations under one of the outbuildings. I can picture the cute little fellows wearing little blue waistcoats, and tiny miner's helmets complete with lamps, Peter Rabbit style. Does anyone have a ferret we could borrow?

Tuesday 8th

As punishment for enjoying the lovely sunshine yesterday, we're subjected to a day of constant rain. It seems that if we want to get any work done around here, we're going to need to grow webbed feet.

We took advantage of the weather to go and visit the aged aunt to collect our redirected post and have a shower. After lunch, we paid a visit to a couple of people we have been meaning to see ever since we got here.

The first shall simply be called Neighbour J. She owns the farm adjoining that of the aged FIL. Well over sixty, she never married, and since her brother died she now lives on the farm on her own. She seems quite content with life though. When we arrived she was guiding two of her four cows into a different field with the aid of a stout wooden stick. A lifetime of work has left her bent nearly double, and she wasn't particularly tall to start with; so in order to employ the customary French greeting method of kissing the cheeks I almost had to kneel. She has the most luxuriant moustache

I've ever seen on a woman, and has happily avoided dentists –
or indeed a toothbrush - for her entire life.

She offered us coffee, and after chatting away happily for
an hour or so, we purposefully happened to mention that we
had planted a couple of elder trees. "Oh!" she exclaimed. "You
like elders? You must have some more. They're an absolute
pest here." She led the way to an overgrown track at the side
of the farm and indicated several young elder trees. "You're
very welcome to take these." She eyed the spade in my hand.
"Oh, good, you have a spade." She eyed the metal washtub
which LSS was carrying. "Oh, good, you have a bucket too.
But that won't be big enough. I'll go and get some plastic
bags."

She trotted off through the rain and returned with three
large plastic fertilizer sacks. Shaking the rain off my hands,
and then drying them surreptitiously on my jeans, I dug the
spade firmly into the soil next to the first sapling, nearly
shattering my wrist as the spade hit major resistance. "Ah,
yes, there's a tarmac road running all the way along here, just
underneath the surface," she explained.

So we now have a galvanized bucket and three plastic bags
full of elders to plant. As soon as it stops raining, that is.

We dropped the bucket, bags and spade off at home, and
then visited the next person on the "To Visit" list.

This was Friend F, someone with whom LSS had once
worked. Last month we were in the village trying to sort out
the domestic assistance for the aged FIL. LSS was using her
mobile phone to speak to someone who had been exceedingly
difficult to contact. Of course her mobile phone battery chose

this particularly important moment in which to expire, so we dashed over to visit the aforementioned Friend F, to beg the use of her phone. Unfortunately once the phone call was over, we had to dash off somewhere else, so it was literally a case of "Thanks for the use of the phone, must dash, we'll catch up later," being called over her shoulder as LSS ran out of the door.

By way of apology we took Friend F a bottle of home-brewed Elderflower Champagne (this is why we like elder trees), and we spent a couple of hours catching up with all the local news. LSS also explained everything that had happened since we'd arrived in France, especially regarding the aged FIL.

We arrived back home at around 9:30 p.m. Still, at least we got some things done today despite the rain; not only do we have some elder trees to plant, we've also now put ticks next to all the names on our "people to visit" list. For the time being, at least.

Wednesday 9th

This morning we waited around for the nurse to visit the aged FIL for his weekly blood test, and then went into town to get his prescription filled at the chemist. Although the aged FIL pays nothing for his medication (as it's all covered by his health insurance), I'm sure his prescriptions are making a substantial contribution to the balance sheet of the local pharmacy. All I know is, my arms are getting tired from carrying the sundry bags of medicines from the pharmacy to the car each week.

Whilst we were in town, we did some food shopping; LSS posted off a cheque to Hyundai France for the *Certificate de Conformité* for her car, and I bought a 35kg bag of cement. Not lime this time, but ordinary grey cement. Oh how excited I was with my purchase! I couldn't wait to unwrap it when I got home. No, not really.

I need to make some concrete foundations for our rainwater recovery system, which will consist of six 510-litre barrels. These will be connected together, but also need to be raised off the ground by about half a metre in order to make it easier to fill a watering can from the tap, or connect a hosepipe. I've decided that the barrels will rest on a platform of wooden planks - well, I say planks; they're actually left-over roof trusses which I spotted in one of the aged FIL's sheds.

The platform will have three brick support columns, which means these columns will each need a concrete foundation because the soil is very soft and sandy. I calculate the total weight of the rainwater storage system to be in the region of 3.5 tonnes.

After a grey start to the day the sun emerged, so in the bright sunny afternoon we planted the elder trees we were given yesterday, and then LSS started the garden; sowing a line of lettuces and a row of radishes. We've already encountered two of the pests with which we will have to deal; a cutworm (which I put in a plastic tray and left on top of a wooden barrel in the hope that a passing bird will find it an attractive snack), and a Colorado beetle. I was fairly sure it was a Colorado beetle, and doing a quick Internet search for photographs of said beetle revealed that it was, in fact, a Colorado beetle.

They love potatoes even more than we do. So we'll need to keep an eye out for these little critters. Apparently you can buy a special preparation to get rid of cutworms; it consists of the bacteria *Bacillus thuringiensis*. I doubt that we're going to be able to find it here though. There doesn't seem to be an effective control for the Colorado beetle; we're hoping that planting rows of marigolds between the potatoes will encourage natural predators like ladybirds - although whether a ladybird larva will tackle a Colorado beetle is a matter which is still up for discussion. I suppose it all depends on how much roadwork and sparring practice it's done.

Thursday 10th

Once again, it has been a lovely sunny day. LSS has progressed with the garden and planted a couple of rows of King Edward potatoes which we brought over from the UK, and a row of French potatoes whose provenance has been lost in the mists of time. (In other words we haven't a clue what sort they are. They were in a box at the aged FIL's place, and he can't remember).

A row of carrots will also hopefully soon be pushing their leafy green foliage above the soil. A couple of pots of specialised tomato seeds have also been started. Some yellow tomatoes with the unlikely name of "Yellow Stuffer", and some which are apparently called "Black Russians". Whether they taste of vodka and coffee remains to be seen.

I cut some more wood into stove-sized pieces, and then sorted out our outdoor bathroom, installing guy-ropes to keep the wooden posts supporting the army groundsheets upright in the face of the prevailing winds.

We celebrated today's labours by having a bath in the late afternoon sunshine. It was absolutely great; and the breeze was pleasantly cooling instead of freezing our wet skin like it did recently.

In the dark recesses of the outbuilding-which-will-eventually-be-the-garage, I came across one of the aged FIL's rifles. It takes .22 short cartridges, which explains the small metal container of these which I found when clearing out one of the cupboards. The rifle is a single-shot type, but the stock is a bit short for me; I guess he'd had it since he was about fourteen or so. Obviously, like everything else he owns, it was extremely rusty. I thought I'd check if it was still working. I checked that the barrel was clear, inserted a cartridge, held the thing at arms' length, pointed it into the garden, cocked the hammer, and pulled the trigger.

Click.

Oh dear. Misfire. Surprise, surprise, not. I cocked the hammer again, and squeezed the trigger. Click. Sigh. For the third and last time, I once more cocked the hammer and pulled the trigger.

Phut.

Ah, ok. I'm afraid this thing would be more useful as a tool for knocking in fence posts. My .177 Diana air rifle would appear to be more powerful. (And more reliable. And more accurate. And there's not a spot of rust on it even though my Dad originally purchased it in 1969, and I inherited it in 1980. I do at least try to look after my possessions).

The rusty rifle has gone into the pile of other stuff which

will be taken back to the aged FIL's house, for him to do with as he wishes.

Today was finally Bramble Revenge Day. As it had been nice and sunny yesterday and today, I thought the pile of bramble debris was looking a bit drier, so went over to it, checked for any hedgehogs (sadly not) and lit a match. Whoof! They were certainly dry enough!

Tomorrow we're off to Blois again to have the ST1100 headlight changed. Hopefully it won't rain overnight - I took a walk along the access lane this afternoon to check if there was any post (there wasn't) and the road is looking much less muddy and slippery than it was last week. The thing I like about living in the countryside, especially after sunset, is the silence. Although if I'm entirely honest, it's not completely silent. Yes, there are no traffic noises or neighbourhood hi-fi systems or televisions. But there is a constant "ribbit-ribbit-ribbit" from the frogs in the pond, the "chirrup-chirrup-chirrup" of the crickets, the occasional call of an unidentified bird, and the "squeeeeeeeech" of a barn owl as it contemplates whether it should deposit its snow-white guano onto the stepladder leaning against the internal garage wall, or onto the garden tools leaning up against the aforementioned stepladder. This all seems to depend on which way the owl is facing at the time.

(Note to self: block up the holes in the eaves of the garage to prevent owls entering. There are several other outbuildings they could use quite happily, so it's not as though it's Owl Discrimination Month).

There are also a profusion of beetles around at present. Excluding the previously-mentioned Colorado beetle, these vary in colour from jet black, through shiny browns and greens, to one particularly catwalk-conscious specimen which had an iridescent green body, and a bright, iridescent pink abdomen.

And the swallows have arrived! I saw one perched on our television aerial this afternoon. A couple of hours later one flew in at the open kitchen door and straight out of the open kitchen window, much to LSS's surprise.

Friday 11th

It didn't rain last night, so the trip to the Honda dealership in Blois was without the slippery incidents of last week. We arrived just before 9:00 a.m., booked the bike in, and then sat and waited. And waited. And waited.

They had a radio station playing over the speakers installed in the showroom; and I wasn't really paying too much attention until my subconscious mind suddenly said, "Er, what was that?" I focussed on the music, and there it was again. A French band, who obviously thought it was cool to use some English words in the refrain of their song. Unfortunately, I didn't quite "get" it.

"On veut du green, green, green, green, green, green washing.

c'est nous les as les pinnochio du marketing.

on veut du green, green, green, green, green, green washing", they warbled.

I listened in amazement, and when we got back home I had to look up the lyrics on the Internet to be sure they had said what I thought they said. They did.

"We want some green, green, green, green, green, green washing.

It is we who are the Pinnochios of marketing.

We want some green, green, green, green, green, green washing."

So there you have it; if you can make more sense out of it than I can please let me know.

Finally at 12:30 p.m. the bike was ready. Well, they were about to close for lunch, so of course they now wanted to get rid of us as quickly as possible. I was presented with the invoice.

Ouch.

The size of the bill meant they were obviously making up for being so helpful last week. 3.5 hours labour to change a headlight? I estimated it would have taken me 45 minutes. Tops. AND I could have found the headlight online for less money. But as previously mentioned, the powers-that-be demand that any work is carried out by an official Honda dealership, and they require duplicate officially-stamped forms to ensure that this is the case. However, interestingly enough, the hourly labour charge was €45 including VAT. In Britain, it was £75. Excluding VAT. Just saying.

Of course whilst we were in Blois, Leroy Merlin attempted to deliver an order we'd managed to place online three weeks ago. (It was for some aluminium five-metre scaffolding; as I'm going to be installing gutters on the house I didn't particularly fancy trying to do this whilst balanced on the top rung of a stepladder; so decided to obtain a proper platform on which to stand.) Having failed to find us at home, the delivery lorry drove to the village, and stopped at the first premises they came to (an agricultural supplies and tractor repair company) to ask for directions to the post office left luggage department. This is where our luck changed. The cashier/administrator/secretary knows LSS; so she told the driver that she would sign for the item, and they could just leave the rather large parcel there. She then telephoned our number, and left a voicemail saying we could collect the parcel at our convenience. This was incredibly helpful of her! I suppose this is one of the advantages of living in a small community - everybody knows everybody!

I spent the rest of the afternoon putting the scaffolding together - it was one of those "Fold Flap A under Tab B and insert into Slot C before installing Bolt D" jobs. But all in French of course. Still, the little pictures came in handy. It's now assembled and at least it looks like the picture on the box. Whilst I was doing this, LSS planted more stuff in the garden including something called salsify which I've never heard of. I presume it's edible.

I'm pleased to report that the fly traps are now fully functional, and gradually filling up with drowned flies. However, flies are still coming into the kitchen. Strangely enough, there aren't any in the aged FIL's house. Mind you, this is probably because he never opens any windows. Not because he wants to prevent any flies entering the house, but because fresh air, like washing, Is Something To Be Avoided At All Costs.

Wildlife diary: Crickets have started making an appearance in the kitchen. They're big black things, and seem to hop in through a hole in the doorframe. Of course they are swiftly helped outside again with the aid of the broom, but generally lose a couple of legs in the process. I know it's just not cricket, but the message does not seem to have spread throughout the cricketing fraternity yet.

Saturday 12th

LSS visited the aged FIL again to try and get him to walk a few steps, with the hidden agenda of doing some laundry in his aged washing machine at the same time. Whilst she was gone, I positioned the newly-assembled scaffolding underneath the hawthorn tree next to the outbuilding-which-will-eventually-be-the-garage with the aim of trimming a couple of the upper branches, because they were growing into the garage roof.

Ooh, I don't like working at heights with a chainsaw. Still, I took my time and am pleased to report that the garage roof is now branch-less.

In the afternoon we went into a shop called "But" in Romorantin. We had received some advertising pamphlets in our post box, and had noticed that they had a special price on a gas oven. Now the one currently in the kitchen is falling apart with rust and only has two gas burners. The other two burners on the hob are electric, as is the oven. Now my Mum had a gas hob-and-oven when I was growing up in South-West-Africa, and in my opinion it's a much more cost-effective method of cooking than using electricity.

Visiting this shop restored our faith in French shopping; as the experience was exactly what we wanted. We went in, and saw the oven. A sales assistant came over.

"May I be of assistance?"

"Yes please, we'd like this oven. Do you have any in stock?"

"Yes we do. Will you be taking it with you today?"

"Yes we will. And we need one of these connector pipe thingies to connect it to a gas bottle."

"Certainly, I'll just print your invoice, you pay at the cashier, and your order will be waiting for you at the counter marked 'Despatch' outside."

Marvellous. Now at last we can finally use all those recipes which say "heat oven to gas mark 5". Installation of the new appliance will need to wait for a while though; we need to clear a space in the "workshop" outbuilding for the old one first. LSS intends using the old stove for making preserves at a later date (rather than filling the kitchen with clouds of steam; it's damp enough indoors already).

On the way home we popped in to a garden centre, and ended up buying some fruit bushes and other plants. A black-currant, redcurrant, some strawberries, two raspberry canes, and some tomatoes. And sundry vegetable seeds as well.

Finally, even though it was a bit windy, we had a barbecue. Pork chops were on the menu this time, and they weren't tough! After dinner, LSS lit the gas burner on the old cooker hob in order to heat some water in the kettle for the washing up. Several minutes later, an odd smell was starting to permeate throughout the kitchen.

"Can you smell burning plastic?" I asked.

"Yes, now that you mention it," LSS replied.

Noses twitching like bloodhounds, we finally found the source. The dinner plates and cutlery had been placed next to the gas hob, with the plastic handle of one of the knives overhanging the heat source. Oops.

This week, LSS has spent considerable time during the weekly shopping trip selecting things for the aged FIL that she thought he'd like to eat, having previously asked him if he fancied anything special.

"No," he had replied. "I'm not fussy."

Unfortunately, this turned out to be more or less a waste of time.

Some bananas: *"Non.* Take those away, I won't eat them."

A minute steak, perhaps? *"Non,* I won't eat it. Take it away."

A *croque monsieur* (toasted ham sandwich)? He ate half of it, then decided it was too hot and he didn't want to eat the rest.

Ham? Too salty. Take it away. *Rillette* (a sort of minced pork paste - he used to like it). Not any more. How about a packet of '*Vache qui rit*' (Laughing Cow) processed cheese slices? He used to like these. No.

Even when it comes to bread - he used to eat eight loaves a week, now he only manages half a loaf. This is unheard of for a Frenchman.

A packet of grated carrots, perhaps? Ah, finally, success. He ate that.

Other than that, he's not fussy. Still, we're not complaining. Our fridge is full.

One lot of foodstuff LSS discovered in the aged FIL's larder was jam. We presumed the jars had been purchased by the late MIL many years ago because the price labels were still in French Francs. We took these back to our house because the aged FIL isn't supposed to eat jam (and this is another of those things he's said he doesn't want to eat anyway).

So, breakfast time arrives, some bread is toasted, and we examine the first jar.

Label: Plum jam. It didn't taste too bad for a 15-year-old jam, I suppose.

Several breakfasts later the pot was empty.

Next pot label: Strawberry jam. Surprise! This was plum jam too. Oh well, we ate it. Several breakfasts later, this pot was also empty. We then looked suspiciously at the third pot. However, this one was conspicuously, reassuringly, comfortingly labelled *"La Confiture d'Amelie. Framboises."* Or in other words, raspberry jam.

Oh no it wasn't. This one was plum jam too. We deduced that the late MIL had made a large batch of plum jam, and had run out of pots. Guess which jam we won't be making for a while?

Sunday 13th

Today we planted the fruit bushes, strawberries and tomatoes that we bought yesterday. I've noticed that rabbits are now trying to assist our house renovation plans by excavating a cellar under the house. However, as they did not request planning permission from us, I regret to advise that these digging operations must cease forthwith.

I had noticed that the aged FIL had a live "humane" rabbit trap in one of his outbuildings, so after visiting him, we brought that back with us. A careful examination revealed that, even though a bit rusty, it still worked. Unfortunately we don't have any carrots yet, so I have just set it up empty in front of one of the rabbit holes in the hope that this particular rabbit will be a bit curious. Or stupid. Or both.

"What's this thing?"

"Can I eat it? No, apparently not."

"Can I hop through it? Oh yes I can."

Snap.

"Oh bugger."

I also brought back a couple of tall metal poles, as LSS has been requesting a washing line for a while now. I dug a fairly deep hole for the first one, set it up, and anchored it to a metal stanchion with some fencing wire. Then I attached the washing line. Unfortunately I then discovered that the distance from the metal post to the side of the outbuilding (where I had drilled a hole and mounted a steel eyebolt) is 10.17 metres. Length of washing line? Ten metres. Oh dear. Still, I used some more fencing wire to make good the shortfall. We'll see if we can buy a longer washing line the next time we're in town.

Wildlife diary: I returned from the half-finished washing line installation to discover an adder (*Vipera berus*) trying to get in under the kitchen door. It was a juvenile, only about 15cm long. Not having my forked stick handy, I picked it up with the ash pan and brush, and carried it to the back of the garden where I threw it carefully into the long grass.

It was very windy again today, so once again we carried the bathtub into the kitchen for our Sunday wash.

Monday 14th

So, the Weldom delivery was due at 11:00 a.m. LSS went to do the aged FIL's washing whilst I cleared a space in the outbuilding-which-will-be-the-garage for the guttering and accessories. I also constructed a temporary table using a wide plank of wood and two trestles. This is to store the lime until it's ready to be used for the plastering; it needs to be kept off the earth floor because this is a bit damp. Well, 11:00 a.m. came and went, and at 11:30 a.m. LSS phoned them.

"Oh, we're terribly sorry, we forgot all about you. We'll try delivering tomorrow."

So, Dear Reader, if you need to do any DIY in France, don't go to Weldom.

Steaming lightly from both ears, LSS stomped off into the garden, taking out her frustration on the few remaining weeds, which didn't stand a chance. After lunch, we drove into town to buy a few more seed potatoes, and visit the aged aunt to collect our redirected mail. No shower today, because we had a bath yesterday. No point in overdoing these things, is there?

On the way back, we stopped at the town's retirement home to collect some forms for the proposed future re-homing plans of the aged FIL. Back at home, LSS then phoned the borehole digger, as it had been a month since we enquired about getting a quote for our own borehole water supply. At the time, we were told that the earliest he could visit us would be some time in June! This has now improved slightly, and we may be able to get a visit towards the end of this month.

At 5:00 p.m. LSS called Weldom again to see what time they would be delivering tomorrow, and was told that the van was now ready and would be leaving in ten minutes. Sure enough, the van arrived within the hour. Finally! We have our guttering! Or so we thought until the driver opened the back of the van.

The only missing items were, in fact, the gutters.

Profusely apologetic, the driver promised to return with the missing items first thing (9:00 a.m.) tomorrow morning. We're not holding our breath.

Wildlife diary: Four fox-cubs playing together in the lane. I was walking to our letterbox to post a letter; they disappeared rapidly into the undergrowth as I approached.

Oh yes, there's a rather nifty postage system here. The inside of your letterbox has a small round bi-coloured dial, white and red. If you need to post a letter, you just put it inside your letterbox and turn the dial so that the red part shows through the little plastic window. When the postman delivers your mail, he takes the letter. As long as you've remembered to put a stamp on it of course!

Tuesday 15th

Time: 8:30 a.m. The Weldom van arrived with our missing gutters from yesterday!

Unfortunately this meant that I was no longer able to pontificate at length to LSS explaining the exact procedure for installing guttering. Instead, I was forced to actually get on with the job. Despite several showers of rain ("Oy! Do you mind waiting until the gutters are installed?"), I am pleased to report that half of one side of the house is now guttered. This was the easy section, as the roof is very low on this side. I didn't even need a ladder.

Tomorrow (after our weekly shopping trip) I will tackle

the slightly higher section of the roof. At least we don't have
to water the garden this evening.

Wednesday 16th

This morning we once again did our weekly shopping, which
included visiting the chemist for another round of the aged
FIL's medicines. I'm starting to think they are beginning to
look forward to our weekly visit, as it was a bit disconcerting
when we were about to enter the pharmacy. A chap in a
striped waistcoat and top hat barred our entry until another
acolyte had finished rolling out a red carpet. He then bowed
profusely and ushered us in, where we were seated in comfort-
able armchairs and offered tea and biscuits. Unfortunately
this was just a daydream whilst we were waiting to be served.
However, this type of treatment would not have been unde-
served; today we ordered the famous *"lit médicalisé"*. Delivery
is scheduled for next Tuesday. Oh won't the aged FIL be
surprised! Especially as he has said he doesn't want it. "The
nurse can just wash me in my own bed," he grumbled. Um,
no, they don't do that. Besides, the doctor has prescribed a
lit médicalisé, so a *lit médicalisé* he's going to get.

We also visited the local DIY store to have a look what
they had in stock, and to see if we could find a kettle. I'm
talking the non-electric variety here; you know - the old type
like a camping kettle, which you can put on a gas hob or wood
stove. Well, we'd looked in the various supermarkets without
success ("Kettles - yes, we have some nice coloured 2 000 Watt
kettles over there. What do you mean, non-electric? ALL
kettles are electric. How are you going to plug in a non-electric
kettle? Don't be silly.")

Well, the DIY store had one. I looked at the price and blinked vigorously. Unfortunately the blinking had no effect; the price tag remained unchanged. €99. Must be because of the "retro" look. Something else we'll need to look for on Amazon.

The afternoon was spent installing guttering, whilst LSS mixed up a batch of nettle surprise.

Recipe for Nettle Surprise:

1 kg of chopped nettles

10 litres of water

Add one to the other (it doesn't matter which way around) and leave for two weeks, stirring every two days until it's stopped bubbling.

Dilute 1:10 and use as a liquid fertilizer.

Note: keep mixture as far away from the house as possible. The surprise is the smell.

LSS and I have started having a tug-of-war for possession of the laptop. We bought this before leaving the UK, and we're very glad we did; using this we were able to check our emails using a dial-up modem before our broadband access was connected. I'm looking forward to sorting out the electricity in the sitting room so that I can plug in the server and each of our computers. At the moment all there is electricity-wise is a sad-looking single plug socket at shoulder height. It's capable of running the printer, router, and Livebox ADSL modem but that's about all. So whilst LSS is using the laptop in the evening, I'm reduced to making diary notes in longhand - and my handwriting is not of the same calligraphic standard it once was.

As the weather was still miserable, we once again had a bath in the kitchen. The water from the ballon is starting to look slightly clearer with fewer rusty flakes in it. It's still pale orange though.

Wildlife diary: On the way back from shopping, an extremely large hare bounded across the road, stared at us in surprise, and as soon as the car had passed, dashed back across the road again from whence it came.

Thursday 17th

Gutters, gutters, gutters. One side of the house is now complete, with the exception of the two downpipes. One of these needs to be funnelled into our waste water system (yet to be constructed) and the other requires the partial dismantling of the outside toilet wall in order to obtain access to the rainwater recovery barrels. In the interim we've utilised one of the large wooden barrels to collect any runoff.

I started the second side of the house, with the aid of the aforementioned scaffolding. Whilst I was climbing up and down ladders, LSS cut the ivy which was beginning to smother the chestnut trees opposite the house. I also gave her a task to do.

<Cue music from Mission Impossible>

"Your mission, should you choose to accept it, is to mark out where the rainwater recovery barrels will go, and dig three holes for the concrete foundations. This message will self-destruct once the rainwater barrels are in place."

Tomorrow's mission: Mixing concrete. Mwuhahahaha.

I also erected the second washing line, as we were able to buy the line in the supermarket yesterday. At least this one was long enough!

Wildlife diary: A large toad. There was a large sheet of rusty metal in the back garden where the rainwater recovery barrels will go, so we removed this. A large toad was underneath and was very unhappy to be disturbed. We left him burying himself in the soil again.

Why on earth the aged FIL left bits of metal all over the garden is anybody's guess. Perhaps he was planning on holding a convention for metal detectorists. The other legacy we're having to deal with on a daily basis is broken glass. It would appear that every time something containing glass was broken, the pieces were just thrown outside next to the house walls. We've taken three bucketfuls of glass shards to the glass recycling bank already, including bits of broken bottles, drinking glasses, phials, window panes, and sundry unidentified bits which could possibly have belonged to spectacles at one stage in their lifetime.

Perhaps all of this was done to deter the Sologne Spectres. These ghostly apparitions are well-known locally for entering isolated farmhouses at night and pulling faces at the inhabitants. However, if there is broken glass at the base of the wall, they cannot enter the house for fear of ripping their white sheets.

No, not really. I made it up.

Whilst I'm on the subject of the aged FIL's various idiosyncrasies, I took advantage of the scaffolding to open up the courtyard external light fitting for the house. Lo and behold, it was half full of the desiccated remains of various bugs. I was initially going to say "cremated remains" but there is no way they could have been cremated; the light bulb was of the 40-watt variety.

Every. Single. Bulb. was 40 watts when we moved in. You couldn't see a thing in the dim glow. Especially in the pantry. But that was different. A fifteen-watt refrigerator bulb had been bodged into the main lighting circuit.

Today was yet another bank holiday, which could explain why the weather for May so far has been dismal. Cloudy, cold and windy in general. Surely that's not normal? We had the wood stove on all day today. But fortunately we haven't had to use any of the wood I'd cut; LSS decided to clear out another of the outbuildings and discovered a cache of bits of firewood underneath some more old oak barrels.

Friday 18th

Once again I worked on the guttering all day. It's so time-consuming because the roof isn't straight, so every gutter-clip support bracket needs to be bent in a slightly different way. I must have walked 15 miles today. Up the ladder, try the bracket, down the ladder, walk to the workshop, bend bracket in vice, walk back to ladder... Still, the second side of the house is nearly complete; with only one two-metre length of guttering still to fit. And the downpipes, of course.

I showed LSS how to mix and pour concrete into the foundation hole she dug yesterday. Two more foundations need to be poured, and then I can build some brick supports for the rainwater barrels. Unfortunately the little taps which came with the barrels are only of use if you want to fill a watering can; you can't connect a hosepipe to them. So a bit of online research showed that plastic taps were available which had an in-built hose connector. What's strange is that we were able to buy six of these taps from an Ebay seller in the UK (including postage) for the price of two of them from Leroy Merlin. I scent a business opportunity!

The potatoes have started poking their leafy shoots through the soil, and the marigolds have also made an appearance; but everything else is being somewhat slow. Mind you, the temperatures have been somewhat below normal for this time of year. It was cloudy and windy again today, but in the evening the sun came out for an hour so we rapidly decided to barbecue some chicken for supper, and very nice it was too.

Wildlife diary: Two large toads this time. I had moved the rusty old dog kennel as it was getting in the way of the scaffolding (to the best of my knowledge there never was a dog in residence!) and they had buried themselves in the soil underneath. I carefully carried each of them to a separate rabbit hole - let's see how the rabbits like their new tenants!

Saturday 19th

The guttering is finally finished! I checked the slope by the simple method of pouring a bottle of water in one end of the gutter, and seeing it trickle all the way along, adjusting the height of the gutter clips as I went. The end section on the south side of the house required me to stand on the roof of one of the outbuildings. In order to do this I decided to use one of the wooden ladders which were stored in the barn (the idea being that laying the ladder flat against the roof tiles it would spread my weight and avoid any tile breakage). The first ladder I disregarded immediately; it is incredibly heavy and is also tied in place (giving access to the loft area above the house). The second looked a better bet, but it seemed a bit light, so I decided to test it out first. I leaned it up against the house wall, and carefully started to climb. The reason for its light weight became apparent as I stood on the third rung; the ladder broke in half due to the activities of - you guessed it - woodworm. It has now joined the other wood-stove fuel material. The third ladder was a home-made one, but was not as old as the others and turned out to be solid enough.

The other task carried out today was to cut more wood for the ever-hungry wood stove, and a much-needed bath in the kitchen was once again enjoyed by both of us; the weather was a bit too windy for our external bathroom. There also wasn't much sunshine!

LSS assisted the aged FIL with his exercise again today. This consisted of walking from the bedroom to the kitchen and back again. Three times. He didn't want to walk any further because the previous time he'd walked more than three circuits, he had an incontinence episode. Of course the fact that he's now on a self-imposed diet of prunes in addition to his normal daily laxative dose had absolutely nothing to do with it.

Wildlife diary: Three fox-cubs playing tag in the field opposite the house. I think when we finally get our chickens we're going to need a stout fence!

Sunday 20th
It rained last night. Not a lot, but sufficient to test the guttering (sigh of satisfaction at a job well done). The gutters

are working fine. Now I just need to connect the downpipes, but this needs to wait until the rainwater barrels are in place. I struggled to find any suitable connectors locally to join the rainwater barrels together; the common-or-garden 20 mm diameter connectors won't do the job because the entire contents of an 80 mm diameter downpipe are entering the barrel.

Elementary school mathematics reveals a problem (if a bath is filled by two taps at a rate of ten litres per minute, and drains away down the plug-hole at a rate of five litres per minute, how long will it take two men to find the missing plug?)

In other words, if the 80 mm diameter inlet pipe is carrying a full capacity of water, it stands to reason that a total diameter of 80 mm is required for the outlet pipe to prevent the barrel overflowing. So the plan is to have a 40 mm diameter pipe joining the barrels, and a 40 mm pipe as an overflow. I was able to find some suitably-sized tank connectors online (again from the UK), and as I already have some lengths of pipe, once the connectors arrive I can join everything together.

Monday 21st

This morning I managed to lay the bricks for one of the foundation pillars for the rainwater barrels, but as I put the last brick in place the heavens opened, and it rained hard for the rest of the day. The gutters are still doing their task; it's just unfortunate that the rainwater barrels aren't connected up yet. I suspect as soon as they're in place and connected, we won't have any more rain for months.

So I moved indoors, and removed the remaining loose wall plaster in the pantry. It's now ready for re-plastering.

Tuesday 22nd

Today I tried my hand at mixing up some lime mortar and filling the deeper holes in the walls where the plaster has come away. It seems to be a very similar methodology to using cement mortar, but much more workable.

I then managed to slice open the ball of my thumb on a broken tile. Where the plaster has come away from the walls in the living room, it has also brought with it a row of tiles which form the skirting. I was chiselling the cement backing off these tiles so that they could be re-used when I managed to break one. For some reason I picked up the broken piece without sufficient care, and discovered that the edge was razor-sharp. Unfortunately the tiny (supposedly) waterproof sticking-plasters which we had in the medicine chest proved insufficient at staunching the flow, so in addition I had to wrap lots of sticky tape around my thumb to avoid getting blood on everything I touched.

LSS spent the entire afternoon with the aged FIL, awaiting the delivery of the famous *"lit médicalisé"*, which finally turned up at around 4:30 p.m. The aged FIL had initially said he didn't want it, but finally gave in under pressure from the doctor. He continues to maintain that he is not actually going to use it.

Needless to say, whilst LSS was away, the borehole man turned up to see if he could determine whether we were suited for a borehole or not. He had been recommended to us by several locals, and was a real water diviner, or dowser. As a result, his services were much in demand so we were fortunate not to have waited longer for an appointment. Fortunately he was of Dutch ancestry, so our conversation took place with a mélange of French, Dutch, and English. He had brought along a piece of string with an odd-shaped bit of metal on the end, a Y-shaped branch, and a can of spray paint.

I watched as he tucked the Y-shaped branch under one arm, and then with the other hand, twirled the string-thing around in various directions. He then attempted to throw it away, all the while keeping hold of one end of the string. He did this several times, and then marched purposefully in one direction, coming to a halt in a patch of long grass. The string-thing was twirled around rapidly again. He then switched to the Y-shaped branch, taking the ends in both hands with the base of the branch pointing straight ahead. He walked slowly forwards and backwards, and it looked as though there was an invisible force pulling strongly on the end of the branch as it seemed to tug his arms downwards in one particular spot. The can of spray paint was now employed; he sprayed an "X" on the grass.

He explained that there was a strong flow of water in that spot; with a rate of flow of around two cubic metres (2 000 litres) per hour, and at a depth of approximately forty metres. He also stated that this was guaranteed; if, for some inexplicable reason, no water was found, we would not be charged a cent.

I was quite pleased about the location of the water source; it's only about fifteen metres from the house. He will be posting us a quote. So this is Section Three of our project list underway (obtain a drinking water supply).

On her return, LSS brought with her one of the aged FIL's lawnmowers, because the grass around the house has liked the rain so much it is now almost waist-high in places. The cat loves it; two steps and she's invisible, much to the chagrin of the mice. I may need to consider fitting the lawnmower with a snorkel due to the amount of rain we're getting at the moment. Mind you, today it didn't start raining until 5:00 p.m.

Wildlife diary: A grey heron in the shallows of the pond, stalking up and down. It was unsuccessful at catching its dinner tonight though, but it must have had some success here in the past because when we first moved in, we found the skeletons of two large carp in the garden.

Wednesday 23rd

In the morning we did our weekly shopping, and stopped off at the aged aunt to have a shower and collect our post. Then in the afternoon I finished the bricklaying for the support columns for our rainwater recovery storage system. Of course this meant I was hot and sweaty; and as LSS had been tackling the brambles, so was she. So we had a bath in the garden in the late afternoon sunshine. Two washes in one day - we feel like we've won the lottery!

The following reminds me of a story I read somewhere a while ago - I don't know how true it is. Some time in the fifties, someone placed an advertisement in the New York Times. "Guaranteed Cockroach Killer! Send in your dollar now!" People that sent in a dollar received, by return post, two pieces of wood, with the instructions to place the cockroach on one piece of wood and hit it with the other. A complaint was received, but no action was taken because the advertisement was not actually misleading. Why this story? Well, tonight LSS and I carried out several Colorado Beetle patrols. These beetles are out in force amongst the newly-sprouted potato plants. We took it in turns to patrol up and down the rows of potatoes, armed with a half-brick and a small piece of roof-tile. We place the Colorado beetle on the small piece of roof-tile and hit it with the brick. Guaranteed results. We must have disposed of well over twenty beetles in the space of an hour or so. Patrols will resume tomorrow, as bad light stopped play.

Wildlife diary: I decided to exclude the Colorado beetles from this as, although they are technically wildlife, they're not welcome. Instead, I chronicle the rescue by LSS of a very bright green 30-cm long lizard from the cat. It was playing dead (the lizard, not the cat). We released it into the garden where it lay motionless, its little sides heaving for breath. We left it alone and when we returned ten minutes later it had gone. So it had obviously run off into the shrubbery. Mind you, the cat was looking rather well-fed. On the other hand, that is her normal appearance.

Thursday 24th

This morning LSS had an appointment in Romorantin with *Pôle emploi* (The Job Centre) as she had been advised to visit them to discuss her proposed assumption of the role of *Auto-Entrepreneur* (Self-employed person to us commoners). This was pretty much a complete waste of time; the staff member was only interested in ticking the neat row of little boxes on the "Client Job Search" form; obviously none of these boxes were ticked because LSS is not actually looking for a job. So the staff member was left moderately unsatisfied, her rows of little boxes still blank. We were also informed that in order to get a job (or even become self-employed), the first thing necessary was to obtain a thing called a *"Carte Vitale"*, the French Health Insurance Card, as without this vital piece of plastic one is unemployable, even by oneself.

We therefore trotted around to the local Social Services offices which issue these.

"Mais non!" the woman behind the counter exclaimed when we explained the reason for our visit. "You first need to be in employment for 90 days before we can issue you with a *Carte Vitale.*" Joseph Heller[2] would have been proud.

Back on the farm, I mixed up another batch of lime mortar and filled some more holes in the pantry walls whilst LSS visited the aged FIL. This was just as well, as it turned out that the domestic assistance lady had not turned up to feed him his lunch. LSS sent an angry email to the domestic assistance company enquiring what the problem was, and is now in possession of the schedule for the next few weeks. Apparently the office was aware that nobody would be turning up today, but the staff member who is responsible for notifying people of the schedules is on holiday, and That Is Her Job And Nobody Else's.

Whilst the mortar was drying, I sharpened the blades of the aged FIL's lawnmower with the aid of my angle grinder, and LSS then trimmed the jungle grass near the pond. Afterwards, we had another much-needed bath in the sunshine in the garden, followed by a barbecue with a couple of well-deserved

---

[2]Author of the book 'Catch-22'

beers. As we had run out of the home-brewed variety we had been reduced to purchasing some run-of-the-mill stuff until such time as my next beer brewing materials arrive. I found it incredibly amusing to discover that bottles of 1664 now carry the following instructions on the label: *"Pour ouvrir, utiliser un décapsuleur adapté"* (To open, use a bottle opener) with a picture of one of these devices. Perhaps Kronenbourg got fed up with being sued by angry Frenchmen saying things like "You didn't tell me I needed to uthe a bottle opener to open my bottle of Thixteen Thixty Four, tho I uthed my teeth. Tho I now have broken inthithorth. What are you going to do about it?"

The Colorado Beetle patrol successfully ambushed and exterminated another two dozen beetles. I found myself walking up and down the rows of potatoes, brandishing the half-brick-and-tile and muttering "Exterminate! Exterminate!" like a Deranged Dalek. I have no idea where all these beetles are coming from.

Wildlife diary: Nothing much to report, unless you include the little brown and grey mouse which the cat brought back proudly at lunchtime to show us, and then promptly ate.

Thursday 31st

I can't believe it's been over a week since my last diary entry. The truth of the matter is we've now fallen into a sort of routine, and unfortunately keeping a diary was one thing which was forgotten. In my defence, I've never been an inveterate diary-keeper in the first place, so it's been a bit of a challenge thus far.

We have started brewing a batch of elderflower champagne, having collected lots of flower heads from Neighbour J's farm. Here's the recipe I use.

Elderflower Champagne Recipe:

Ingredients:

350g flowers with as many of the green stalks removed as possible

8 litres water

1.75kg sugar

1 lemon

20g citric acid

5g wine yeast

1 campden tablet

1 tsp Yeast nutrient

Method:

Heat 4 litres water with sugar in a large saucepan. Remove from heat as soon as the sugar has melted.

Add the washed flowers and mash with the back of a spoon.

Add 4 litres cold water, lemon juice and zest, and citric acid.

Mix well and leave covered for 24 hours.

Strain into a fermentation vessel.

Add campden tablet. Leave for 24 hours.

Add heating belt if temperature of liquid is below 20 degrees Centigrade.

Add yeast nutrient and yeast, stir, and then seal the fermentation vessel (with an airlock in place).

Leave until fermentation stops.

Rack, and then bottle in sterilized bottles to each of which half a teaspoon of sugar has been added.

Keep for 2 weeks before drinking.

Work is still progressing on the house. I'm just waiting for a final Ebay order of the tank connectors for the rainwater barrels. We also searched the local shops for an adjustable hole cutter (so that I can cut an 80 mm diameter hole in one of the barrels for the downpipe entry) and finally gave up, ordering this item online as well.

We've also managed to have a bath every day for over a week now - mind you, we've needed it as most of the work we've been doing has created a lot of dust. I'm pleased to report I managed to clear a space in the woodshed, and made An Important Find. I discovered four large 44-gallon drums (210 litres if you've gone metric) with removable lids! These could come in very handy for making charcoal at a later date. Basically you fill the barrel with wood, put the lid on tight (installing a pipe to let gases escape) and light a fire under the barrel. The wood inside is thus cooked, converting it to charcoal. And as a bonus, you can use the gases coming out of the pipe for fuel as well - either for cooking or running an engine. During the Second World War many vehicles were converted to run on wood gas.

The war on the Colorado Beetles is progressing, and I think the tide has finally turned. Every day last week we were getting around thirty beetles. This number has fallen over the past couple of days to thirteen, and today was an all-time low of seven.

We also visited Castorama in Orleans yesterday, and spotted a wooden porch at a knock-down price of around €40. This will come in very handy to protect the kitchen door from the rain. Today's shopping consisted of visiting Leroy Merlin in St.Doulchard (about 40km away). The aim was to purchase some paint and also a double-glazed PVC window (we have three more to order but I want to see how easy they are to install before purchasing the rest). The window we bought is for the kitchen, and the aperture measures 1042mm in height by 1085mm width. Without having a window custom-made, the closest size displayed in the catalogue and on Leroy Merlin's website was 1050mm high by 1000mm wide. I was fairly sure this size would do the job, with a bit of chiselling of the cement window surround at the bottom, and a bit of filling in at the sides.

Taking my trusty tape measure with us, we measured the actual window before buying. Its actual measurements were 1050mm in height by 1065mm in width. I've no idea why they measured the width incorrectly. The good news is it will fit even better than we thought. We've also been attacked by what we think must be fleas. The cat has now been banned from the bedroom, and is Not Happy. The bed linen has been washed at the hottest temperature the washing machine can provide, and the mattress sprayed with some anti-tick, anti-flea, anti-bedbug, anti-pretty-much-everything stuff. Despite examining ourselves, and the bed, and the cat, closely, we have not found a single flea. So possibly all our itchy bites are from mosquitoes (there are quite a lot around). We're now caked head to toe in bug repellent. I just wanted to make you aware life on La Darnoire is not always entirely rosy!

I've also been occupied with registering domain names and all that sort of stuff, ready for setting up the website about the property renovation.

Last Friday was a day which will henceforth be known as "The Day of the Great Pepper Pot Disaster."

LSS had made a salad for dinner, consisting of lettuce, cubes of ham, cucumber, tomatoes, and sliced crab sticks. She had already added the vinegar and oil, mayonnaise and salt, and the last thing to go in was a sprinkle of pepper. I was in the garage at the time, and heard an anguished "Oh la la", with a pronunciation that only a French person could achieve. Upon investigating the reason for this cry, it appeared that the lid had fallen off the pepper pot at first shake, with the result that the salad bowl consisted of an amorphous mound of grey stuff. I made the mistake of trying to blow some of the pepper away. I now know what it feels like to be on the receiving end of a pepper spray.

"Maybe it won't be too bad," I said, scraping some pepper off what I think was a piece of cucumber and popping it into my mouth to test.

Yuk.

To cut a long story short, the salad was finally rescued by washing the whole lot, and LSS adding more vinegar, oil and mayonnaise. Upon tasting, it was quite nice. However, my quip of "Hmm, very tasty. Needs pepper though." was met with a stony glare, and I have not been the flavour of the month since. I have therefore kept out of the way, keeping myself occupied with fitting out my workshop by clearing some space against one wall, laying some concrete foundations (no bricks this time!) and installing my workbench. Of course there's no power or lighting in the workshop yet but there will be, oh yes there will be.

June

A tornado damages the other farmhouse, but also supplies us with lots of firewood. I discover how to make charcoal, and Cat brings us a pheasant for dinner. A new double-glazed window is installed in the kitchen, and the electricity re-wiring starts.

Friday 1st

LSS spent several hours at the aged FIL's, for the first time meeting the person in charge of a service called SSIAD. This is a sort of domestic medical hygiene service, and LSS has been trying to get their assistance for over a month now. (It's not right that a daughter should be washing her own father). Not that much washing has taken place thus far though; a quick lather of the legs and upper body has taken place on Saturday afternoons but that's as far as it went. The good news is that SSIAD will now take over this service, and not only that, but the aged FIL will now be thoroughly washed daily (excepting weekends). He will never have been so clean. (Even the physiotherapist who visits three times a week had started commenting that he truly was a smelly old man).

I filled in the hole in the floor in the outbuilding containing the infamous *ballon*; the hole was dug years ago to insert the pipe leading to the well and was never filled in. We got fed up with falling into it, so today another little job was ticked off the list. We also erected a trellis fence next to the pea plants which have started to sprout - at least the little things will now have something to climb onto!

Today's Colorado Beetle count: three. I have also initiated a new sport, Ladybird Relocation. The rules are simple; search the garden for a ladybird (there are plenty). Encourage it to climb onto your finger. Then run like mad to a plant infested with greenfly (for example one of the little peach trees) and encourage the ladybird to climb off your finger onto a greenfly-covered leaf. I successfully transplanted five before getting bored. Knowing the voracious appetites of ladybirds, I'm fully expecting the peach tree to be greenfly-free by tomorrow morning.

Wildlife diary: A roe deer crossing the farm track. We also now have a stuttering cuckoo in the neighbourhood, which sounds very odd indeed. The call is something like: cuckoo, cuck-oo, cuck-cuck-cuck-cuck-cuck-oooooo (the last few syllables in a frenzied crescendo).

Saturday 2nd

I can't get over how expensive paint is in France. The last time we were in Leroy Merlin I was astonished - an external gloss paint for wood is around €49 per litre!

Today I poured a small test foundation for the barn wall. It's a double-thickness wall which is fortunate, because the two lower courses of bricks on the outside of the wall have crumbled into nothingness along its entire length. The idea is to put a small foundation in place before replacing the two lower courses of bricks. Because it's a very old farmhouse, it's not a good idea to introduce cement; so I'm doing everything with NHL 3.5 lime. The mixture I used was one part lime, two parts sand, and two parts gravel. It seemed to work all right, but I need to leave it for a while to set before I can lay bricks on it. This is the one disadvantage of using lime; it sets much more slowly than cement.

I also progressed in sorting out some bits and pieces in the workshop, and filled the remainder of the holes in the pantry walls; these are now ready for rendering. I tried some of LSS's elderflower cordial which she made a couple of days ago and bottled today. Very nice it is too; she may make some more tomorrow. The elderflower champagne which I've started brewing has still not started fermenting, so I suspect the temperature in the house is just too cold for the yeast. I'll leave it alone for a few more days.

Tomorrow there's a car boot sale in Lamotte Beuvron which we'll go and have a look at.

Elderflower Cordial Recipe:
Ingredients to make 4 litres of cordial:
15 flower heads with as many of the green stalks removed as possible (do not wash)
2 litres water
2kg sugar
Juice of 2 lemons
40g citric acid

Method:
Bring the water to the boil.
Place the flowers in a large bowl and pour the boiling water over them.
Add the lemon juice and cover.
Macerate this mixture for 2 to 4 days at room temperature, stirring occasionally.

Strain through a sieve into a large saucepan and add the sugar.

Heat, and stir until the sugar has dissolved.

When the liquid begins to boil, remove from heat and add the citric acid.

Stir well, then pour the cordial into sterilized, warmed bottles.

Cork the bottles and allow to cool (screw-top bottles may be used).

Store in a cool place, and keep in the refrigerator once opened.

Sunday 3rd

The car boot sale was pretty dismal; it was raining and there weren't that many stalls. On the way back we stopped at the aged aunt's house, and she invited us to stay for lunch.

Monday 4th

Today I decided to try my hand at making charcoal. I constructed a retort using a small oil drum from which I removed the top. I cleaned out the remaining oil as best I could, then packed it with pieces of oak and covered it with the lid from an old paint container, which happened to fit pretty snugly. The drum was then inserted into an empty 210-litre drum which was already seeing service as an incinerator. I filled the gap between the two drums with cardboard and smaller pieces of wood, then set fire to it. I kept the fire going for three hours, then let it die out naturally. During the burn, one could see jets of wood gas escaping from the lid of the smaller drum and igniting with a muffled roar. I'll let it cool down overnight and have a look tomorrow.

Tuesday 5th

We have charcoal! I'm feeling very pleased with myself indeed.

LSS started making another batch of elderflower cordial, and a chap came around to discuss our options for getting the water from the future borehole into the house. He had been recommended to us by the water diviner, and he does a lot of work with them. Unfortunately, due to current building regulations, it seems we'll require another of the famous *"ballons"* to store the water. I explained that it would be located upstairs, which he thought was rather unusual until I explained our lack of living space.

"I see," he said. "But, of course, you'll need to drain the system completely in the winter."

"Why?" I asked, puzzled.

"Because the water will freeze and burst the pipes. Or the *ballon.*"

"But we'll insulate it properly," I objected. "And if the system is empty, what exactly are we supposed to use as a water supply in winter time?"

He regarded me with surprise.

"You mean you're actually going to *live here?*" he asked.

There must be something about this area that people have not told us. Did it have a bad reputation for wolves during winter? Was there perhaps some swamp-monster, quiescent during the warmer months, which appeared as soon as the temperature dropped?

"Of course we're going to live here!" I answered.

"Oh, I'm sorry. I thought this was going to be a summer holiday home. Well, as the house will be heated during the winter, you shouldn't have a problem."

He'll send us a quote for the work required.

LSS moved some of the kitchen furniture around a bit so that more of the wall space could be de-greased, de-moulded, and otherwise cleaned prior to being painted. We've devised a Cunning Plan for freeing up some space in the (small) kitchen. I'll build a brick cupboard with a lockable door outside against the kitchen wall. This will be accessed from the inside by means of a hatch, and the cupboard will not only store the gas cylinder for the hob/oven, but firewood for the wood stove. The firewood is currently being kept in a metal cupboard which the aged FIL appears to have constructed from the shell of an old washing machine. He is hereby awarded a gold star for economical recycling.

Wednesday 6th

I forgot to mention that there were no Colorado Beetles on the potatoes at all yesterday. Today there were only three. So it looks like we're winning the battle, but I don't think we can organise a Victory Parade just yet.

I re-plastered part of the pantry wall using lime render, and LSS started painting one wall of the kitchen with a white primer coat. It already looks tremendously improved; the previous dingy brown paint made the kitchen look even smaller than it is.

The adjustable hole saw which I bought from Ebay arrived in the post, so I was able to drill two 82mm diameter holes in two of the water barrels so that the rainwater downpipes can go into the barrels in the right places.

The elderflower champagne still hasn't started fermenting, so I've had to order a brewing belt. This is a device which plugs into the mains, and you wrap it around the brewing container (either the plastic bucket or a demijohn) to provide the correct temperature for yeast to do its job. Obviously our previous house in Reading had central heating, so the temperature was fine for home brewing. La Darnoire, however, has no heating at all, and even though the temperature outside has now risen, it's still below twenty degrees in the house itself.

Thursday 7th

We did our weekly shopping this morning, including the usual visit to the chemist for the aged FIL. Fortunately (yes, fortunately) they were out of stock of the usual heavy items, and LSS put her foot down, saying we were NOT coming back in the afternoon to collect these; they could jolly well deliver them.

A suitably chastened chemist agreed that they would be delivered tomorrow, by post. Upon our return home, LSS drove off to the aged FIL to deliver his shopping. The sky had clouded over and there was a constant thundering noise. I had just started mixing some lime render for the pantry when a) the electricity cut off and b) there was a sudden storm. I stood by the kitchen window looking out at the lashing rain, which the strong wind was driving horizontally. A few hailstones fell as well, but this didn't last long.

Much to my surprise, ten minutes later LSS screeched to

a halt outside and dashed indoors. "Are you all right?" she asked.

"Er, yes, why shouldn't I be?" was my surprised response.

"Because we've just had a tornado. The other farmhouse was hit, there are trees down everywhere, and there aren't any tiles left on the roof!"

I jumped in the car with her and we scooted over to the aged FIL's house. I found there had been a slight exaggeration; there were about twenty roof tiles missing (which of course meant that the rainwater had poured into the upper floor and was now dripping from the oak beams into every room). Buckets were scattered everywhere, catching the drips. One of the outbuildings was worst hit: a three metre section of ridge tiles and a fairly large area of surrounding roof tiles were missing. A large oak tree had given up the contest and was lying on its side in a field, several broken branches had flattened the fence surrounding the kitchen garden, and a smaller tree had fallen across the access road. I drove back to La Darnoire to fetch the chainsaw and cleared the road. The branches were removed from the fence, and then I assisted in sweeping up a lot of fallen ceiling plaster.

Crisis over, I left LSS telephoning the insurance company on behalf of the aged FIL (the telephone was still working) and returned home, where I fished out several large branches from the fishpond. I discovered that the scaffolding had blown over, but there was no other damage.

Wildlife diary: Whilst removing the branches from the pond, I discovered that the duck had returned, and had constructed another nest in which there were ten eggs. Hopefully she has better luck with this batch.

Friday 8th

Well, the postman did bring the aged FIL's prescription today, so he was happy (the aged FIL, not the postman, who had to drive his post-van over the potholed road to deliver the 24 bottles of booster food supplements. I'm just glad that for once I didn't have to carry the stuff). These food supplements are bottles of liquid prescribed by the doctor in order to try and increase the aged FIL's calorie intake, as he's not eating enough. Unfortunately, once he's had one of the bottles, he tends to lose his appetite. So we're trying to get him to drink one after each meal, not before, as he insists on doing.

Today's work schedule was completely avoided. Instead of doing what was on the list of jobs, I borrowed the aged FIL's tractor. I first had to fill it up though - not with farm diesel, but with transmission oil - it has a bad oil leak and goes through two litres of 80W90 every time you use it. (The following unfortunately can't count for the wildlife diary; I discovered a dormouse which had fallen into an open bucket of old engine oil, poor thing). I also borrowed some heavy chains, the reason for which will become apparent shortly.

At the end of the property, a tree had blown down in yesterday's high winds, blocking the road. It's not a very heavily used road, but I didn't pass up the chance of some free wood, so pootled (technical term) down the lane with the tractor and chainsaw. I cut up the main trunk first (it was a fifteen-metre tall aspen) and put the logs into the transporter box on the back of the tractor. However, the crown of the tree had hung up in the branches of the trees on the opposite side of the road. This is where the heavy chains came in. I tied the chain around the trunk, and hooked the other end over the front tow bar of the tractor. Selecting reverse second gear, I backed off slowly, and much to my surprise the entire upper part of the tree was pulled free. It must have weighed well over a ton, but I was seriously impressed with the pulling power of the tractor.

I also cut up two smaller wild cherry trees which had unfortunately blown down, and spent the afternoon splitting the logs with a splitting maul. LSS had gone to the aged FIL after lunch in order to do some washing, and I took the tractor back, parking it in its customary place in the barn. The chains needed to be returned to the workshop building, and the only way to carry all of them was to drape some over each arm, and over each shoulder. This resulted in the most amazing clanking noise as I walked, so I took a detour past the kitchen, rattling the chains and calling out "Oooooo, Ebeneeeeezer Scroooooooge. This is the ghoooost of Jaaaaacob Maaaaaarley." Unfortunately my acting skills were completely wasted, as nobody was there.

Completely tired out from the day's labours, we decided to go to a restaurant for dinner. We went to a Chinese place in Salbris where they served an all-you-can-eat buffet for €15 per head, and very nice it was too.

Saturday 9th

I split and stacked more wood. Oh my aching back! They say wood warms you twice; once when you cut it, and the second time when you burn it. It certainly does!

A chap called Fawlty (no, really, that was his name - only in reality it's spelled slightly differently) came to the other farmhouse today to cover the outbuilding roof with a tarpaulin. I'm not sure if he had an assistant called Manuel or not. "¿Que?"[3]

I also cleared some more fallen branches at the corner of the fence near the pond, and then we had a barbecue using our home-made charcoal which worked very well! We may be able to sell bags of it to passing cyclists from the local campsite, Les Alicourts. (This is a large campsite not far from us, frequented by fairly large numbers of Dutch, Belgians, Germans and English). Only three Colorado Beetles today (there were none yesterday).

I also repaired the splitting maul which I managed to break yesterday; the handle snapped off just below the head. My excuse is that it was pretty damaged in that area before I started using it! (And the axe will probably follow suit shortly, there's not much wood in the socket of the axe head). I simply cut off the damaged piece of the handle and re-shaped it to fit the head of the maul. (I can recommend the "Piranha", which is a disc of coarse sandpaper which fits on an angle grinder). Lacking any proper iron wedges, I then inserted a large diameter screw into the end of the handle to expand the wood in order to grip the head of the maul securely. The maul, axe, and my own small axe were then sharpened, again using the angle grinder, ready for the next batch of wood! Actually

---

[3]This is a reference to a television comedy in Britain, called "Fawlty Towers"

this will probably be the large oak tree which was felled by this week's tornado.

Sunday 10th

It rained all day. We took advantage of this to give each other a haircut. Oh yes - and the cat brought us a gift of a pheasant. It was a very pleasant pheasant present. It was a fairly old bird, and having dug out my CSI kit from the barn and donned a deerstalker hat, with the aid of a large magnifying glass I set out to track the scene of the crime. I didn't have to track the trail of feathers very far, as it happens.

We deduced that the bird was probably half-blind with old age, and had flown smack into one of the chestnut trees across the lane. The cat had simply dragged it from there into the front garden. So as it was a fairly cool day, we lit the wood stove, and the pheasant spent the afternoon bubbling away in the *Le Creuset* cast-iron cooking pot.

That was supper taken care of - with very low food mileage indeed; in fact the distance this particular food travelled was approximately ten metres. This includes the garden-grown potatoes we ate with it. The green beans had travelled a bit further - a kilometre - as they came from the other garden. Ah yes, unfortunately we don't know how far the onions had travelled, because we bought those. They were probably from New Zealand.

Monday 11th

The morning was spent preparing the kitchen for the installation of the new PVC double-glazed window which we bought from Leroy Merlin last week. We really must get a trailer for the car; the window we bought only just fitted into the back with the rear seats folded down. Thank goodness it's a hatchback.

In the afternoon we went into a nearby village to enquire about changing the headlights on the Hyundai for French ones; this seemed to be a fairly painless process because the chap in charge of the garage we visited had been through this process before for another English family. However when he called the closest dealership to order the parts, the person he spoke to could not understand why both headlights needed to be changed. "Are they broken?" he asked. When informed that the headlights were in working order, but needed to be converted for driving on the right, he seemed to be astonished that there were some countries that did NOT drive on the right. (This conversation was deduced from our overhearing the replies given by the garage chap to questions posed by the dealership).

We also asked about fitting a tow bar, and were told this was not a problem.

We're still working our way through the contents of the late MIL's pantry (the aged FIL doesn't eat any of the stuff in there). Tonight we had some baked potatoes with a Bolognese sauce. The sauce contained two pots of home-preserved tomato sauce dated 1997. Fifteen years old!

Almost a vintage!

But it was very tasty, and tehre hvae bin no efter afficts it ull.

Tuesday 12th

For the new kitchen window, I constructed two replacement side frames out of some scrap timber (the only bits I could find which were not riddled with woodworm, and of suitable length), and LSS gave them a coat of wood primer. These side frames are necessary because not only is the replacement PVC window slightly narrower than the aperture, but the existing wood frame also supports the metal shutters on the outside.

We've had so much rain recently that the two rainwater barrels which receive the flow from the gutters have had to be emptied three times. This has been done by the simple expedient of connecting the hosepipe to each tap in turn, and running the other end of the hosepipe down to the pond. We're having to do this because the fittings to connect all six barrels together have still not turned up.

Wildlife diary: I finally caught a sight of the barn owl which appears to be nesting in the roof of the garage. I wouldn't mind it roosting there if only it stopped leaving its white guano all over the workbench.

Wednesday 13th

The husband of an old school friend of LSS is a carpenter (*menusier*), so we had asked him to pop around to give us a quote for a couple of replacement doors. The problem is that the current doors are not standard sizes, so we can't just buy off-the-shelf replacements and stick them in. We also asked him to quote for a sliding door for the pantry. Using a sliding door will free up most of one wall for shelf space.

So this morning I removed the original pantry door and frame and lime-rendered the gaps left by the frame. The pantry already looks much bigger, because the dark brown inward-opening door really blocked the light, as well as making most of one wall unusable.

Thursday 14th

After having done our weekly shopping in the morning, not only was there no prescription to collect for the aged FIL (so our shopping was completed in record time) but we were delighted to discover that today's post contained the missing rainwater barrel connectors! So the rest of the day was spent installing these. Section one of the project list is complete! (Gutters and Rainwater Recovery). We can consider Section two as complete as well (The Garden) although this will be an ongoing activity.

Speaking of the aged FIL, his mood has improved tremendously recently. I wonder if his daily wash could have anything to do with it? He has even offered to pay for the borehole installation. Well I suppose technically, as he's still the owner of the property, he may be feeling some landlordly-type guilt? Maybe not. But we're certainly not going to argue.

LSS started clearing the upper floor of the house which contained all sorts of rubbish. This meant there was another pile of wood (woodworm-infested old rafters for example) to cut up with the chainsaw. She also discovered an old barn-owl nest, and a large pile of chestnuts which had been there for decades, still in their outer spiky shells. It's highly unlikely any of these were edible, as most appeared to have wormholes in them. They all went into the brazier bin ready for heating the next batch of charcoal.

The sun came out in the afternoon so we managed to get a dose of much-needed vitamin D. We celebrated this by eating the six garden strawberries which were now fully ripe. We've also started enjoying the radishes; we had some of these at lunchtime and they are much more peppery than the sort you can buy in the supermarkets. I'm looking forward to the day when the watermelons are ready to eat!

Friday 15th
We received a quote for the installation of a water pressure vessel (ballon) and the connecting of the pipe work from the future borehole to the house. As a result, I have been researching online prices for this equipment, and have found that we'll be able to do it ourselves for less than half the price of the quote. No real surprise there. Apart from the sundry plumbing fittings and copper pipes, we also need a 200-litre pressure vessel, and a twenty-metre length of 32mm diameter thick-walled PVC pipe. This can be obtained locally.

Monday 18th
We've had a very busy weekend, which is why there were no diary entries for the past two days.

On Saturday, I finally registered the domain name for the property's website, www.la-darnoire.com, and I uploaded the first few pages.

Whilst I was doing this, LSS painted the pantry with a white all-purpose undercoat. Everything was painted except the floor. (Even the roof-beams got a coat - after having been cleaned of thirty years' worth of grime first). LSS was so thorough, that when she stood still, she blended perfectly with the background. In other words, she was covered with paint as well.

When she had finished, I removed the kitchen window entirely, enlarged the opening slightly at the top and bottom with a hammer and chisel, and fitted the new PVC window. Actually, I used more than a hammer and chisel. The bottom of the window opening had been cast in concrete. But this was no ordinary concrete; it would not have been out of place in a nuclear fallout shelter. Hard? You have no idea. I finally resorted to my ultimate weapon - my trusty DeWalt angle grinder. But I used no ordinary cutting disc. In my armoury was a diamond-studded mortar raking wheel (which I bought many years ago to chase a channel into a wall). This did the job in record time. However, when I switched off and turned around, the house was a) quiet and b) invisible. LSS was standing outside in the garden with eyes as big as saucers. I could only just see her through the dust. And of course one of the first things we did when we moved in was to remove the interior door separating the kitchen from the lounge. Oh dear. Dust covered everything.

Still, at least the opening was now big enough for the window. However, as I had made the wooden uprights for the frame on both sides out of scrap timber, the sides were not of uniform thickness, which meant they had to be removed again and run through the radial arm saw to even them up. But the window was finally in place, and it makes a big difference to the level of light entering the kitchen.

Yesterday we re-measured the pantry with the aim of covering all of the wall space with shelving. My idea was to mount steel uprights on each wall, and then have shelving brackets supporting 18mm MDF shelves. However, when we added up the costs, the total came to over €500! As LSS pointed out, this was not in keeping with our motto of doing things as cheaply as possible. But short of re-using a pile of old bricks, and scrounging lots of old pallets which could be cut up for shelving, we were a bit stuck.

However, LSS spotted some plastic garage shelf units in the Castorama catalogue, priced at €40. Each shelf is capable of supporting 80kg in weight - and the sizes were just what we needed. But as we had planned to visit BricoDepot in Saint-Germain-du-Puy today anyway, we thought we'd see if they had anything similar. And they did! So we bought three shelf units, and I also stocked up with sundry items like wood screws and Fischer plugs, and the total came to €159. Now that was more like it! (If there had been any scrap wood lying around we would have used it, but it's all infested with woodworm. And aside from that, the pantry is quite damp, so plastic shelving is just the ticket for this sort of environment).

Yesterday I also took advantage of the brazier bin being full of rubbish from the loft, and made another barrel-load of charcoal. Also, Friend L popped in to see us. She's an old college friend of LSS, and was suitably impressed with our efforts to date, being no slouch herself when it comes to DIY. She even hand-builds her own kayaks. In fact it was due to her recommendation that we visited BricoDepot. LSS's home-made elderflower cordial was tested and approved, as was our home-brewed cider from last year.

Wildlife diary: Mrs Jemima Puddle-Duck is still in residence on her nest.

Tuesday 19th

Today I applied the lime render to the newly-installed PVC window surround, including the upper frame which was a complete nightmare. Lime plaster is heavy. And stuffing it into a vertical crack means it falls out faster than you can put it in. LSS came to the rescue, using her smaller fingers to pack it in solidly. She then patched the remaining holes in the pantry walls and repainted the non-patched bits.

We also received the quote for our two doors; the kitchen door and the front door. The menusier had forgotten that we'd asked about a sliding door for the pantry, which was probably just as well. Are you sitting down? The quote was nearly €2500. I think this is another little job I'll have to do myself.

Wednesday 20th

We think we've found out why it's such a struggle to buy anything here, with high prices and nobody having the item you want in stock. It's because companies are actually taxed on the amount of stock they hold. So it stands to reason, to pay less taxes, they reduce the amount of stuff they have for sale. It's mad. Absolutely mad. How NOT to promote business. And yet France is not in recession whilst Britain is? I think they've fudged the figures. Either that or the rest of the world is buying lots of French cheese. And champagne. And perfume. And L'Oreal. And......

Thursday 21st

Item five on our main project list (upgrading the electricity wiring) has been under investigation. The main supply to the property is three-phase. This means there are four wires exiting EDF's meter box; one blue wire (neutral) and three red wires (each carrying a live supply of 220V). Unlike in Britain, where doing any electrical work is Frowned Upon, in France the wiring you're not allowed to touch is anything belonging to EDF. In other words anything up to and including the meter box. From that point on, it's up to you. Now I'd only ever worked on single phase electricity before, so three-phase was a brand new animal to me. Fortunately, one of LSS's cousins is married to an electrician, so we could just ask him to pop around and give us some advice. Or so we thought. They have indeed popped around twice, but as soon as we mention the word "electricity", the subject is rapidly changed.

This is actually understandable, as the same sort of thing has happened to me in the past when I worked in IT. As soon as someone heard what I did for a living, they would start off by describing in minute detail just what it was that had stopped working on their own computer. Carefully worded questions then reveal that they've tried to install a friends' copy of an operating system on a pc which should be in a museum. I became tired of people asking me to do computer diagnosis and repair in my free time.

So it is really up to me to research the best way of upgrading the electricity supply.

Friday 22nd

Today I started the construction of a display table for my bonsai trees. Yes, that's another hobby of mine. Where do I find the time? I sank some creosote-treated telephone pole sections into the ground, and fixed a long wooden beam on top with screws. Very Japanese it looks too. To protect the table from insects and the weather, I painted the whole thing with old engine oil. It does the job, it's cheaper than paint, and there's a whole drum of the stuff at the aged FIL.

We also had a barbecue, and LSS made us a salad containing purslane leaves (a weed growing all over the garden). Its Latin name is *Portulaca oleracea*. We used to grow this in our flowerbeds in Namibia because it is a drought-resistant plant and looks pretty, but I never knew you could eat it!

LSS also started painting the metal shutters of the replaced PVC window. Once they're dry I'll put them back and we'll see what it looks like with white shutters instead of rust-red ones.

The Village Council cut the grass in the lane today using a tractor with two mower attachments. At least, it's their responsibility to keep the roads clear, but I don't think any of them do the work themselves, so this chap was probably a hired contractor.

Oh yes, and first thing this morning LSS took the Hyundai to a local garage, and the headlights were changed to right-hand drive ones in an hour. (Compare this to the three hours it took Honda in Blois to change one motorcycle headlight). She also enquired about the price of a tow bar, but on discovering that it was five times more expensive than buying it online, she wisely chose the latter option. Of course this means I will probably need to dismantle the rear of the car in order to fit the thing.

Saturday 23rd

Yet more research was done into the upgrading of the electricity wiring. The first thing we'll need is a thing called a three-phase *parafoudre*. Because there are occasional summer storms in this area, with lots of lightning, this object prevents all your electrical equipment from damage if lightning strikes one of the main supply pylons. It's like a heavy-duty trip-switch. Of course neither this house nor the aged FIL's has one of these at present, which means whenever a storm threatened, the aged FIL used to run around unplugging everything, having learned the hard way that refrigerators and televisions do not like umpteen thousand volts of electricity.

Sunday 24th

With the engine oil now dry on the newly-constructed display stand, I installed my eight Bonsai trees in their new home. Each is securely fastened to the table with a length of wire through the root ball, so they are not in danger of being blown over. Six of them are pines, which were grown from seed. There is also a juniper, and that old Bonsai favourite, a Japanese maple. It remains to be seen whether they like their new country or not.

Monday 25th

LSS and I went to the Chamber of Commerce in Blois this morning to attend an advertised lecture on How To Start Your Own Business In France. To be honest, I very much doubt that any of the attendees came away from the lecture fired with enthusiasm. Nobody in their right mind would want to start their own business in France if they followed all the instructions to the letter; there's just too much red tape.

On the way back we stopped at the BricoDepot hardware shop where I bought some electrical supplies; they didn't have everything that I needed but - a massive surprise - when we got home I managed to find a website

a) in France with
b) free delivery that
c) had everything that I wanted in stock at
d) very reasonable prices.

So who was this paragon of French electrical DIY? Bis Electric. Not only that, but I was able to discover the difference between an *Interrupteur Différentiel* type A and type AC. We will need two type A's and one type AC. I'm sure you can't wait to find out what the differences are between these. Well, they are both circuit breakers, but the type A protects the circuit from surges of both alternating current and direct current, and is generally used in a circuit on which there is equipment containing electronic circuit boards; things like computers, dishwashers, or washing machines, for example. Type AC only protects the circuit from surges of alternating current, so this one will be used to protect the circuit for the workshop. All very exciting stuff!

Tuesday 26th

Today I cut the grass alleyways between the stands of trees around the property using the grass-cutting attachment on the back of the tractor. We initially struggled to connect the three-arm system to the back of the tractor; but M&O turned up to show me where they wanted the grass cut most urgently, and with their aid the grass-cutter was soon attached.

The next step was to discover which of the myriad of levers and pedals in the tractor made the main power take-off driveshaft turn. I finally found the lever, and in the process also discovered both the diff-lock pedal (which could come in handy one day) and the hand throttle, which meant I could set the engine speed manually and then just sit there and steer. Much progress was made; I estimate nearly half of the lanes have now been mowed.

When I had finished for the day, I parked the tractor in its barn, and when I opened the door, hundreds of horseflies flew OUT. They had been keeping me company in case I got lonely. I look a bit like Frankenstein's monster except I'm not yet green. Reason: two separate horseflies have bitten me on both sides of the neck, pretty much evenly below the ears, so the swollen areas make it look as though I have a bolt holding my head on.

Tomorrow I'll need to use the chainsaw to get rid of two more fallen trees which are blocking one of the lanes (more firewood!) and I should then be able to get on with cutting the rest of the grass. The reason for cutting this grass is two-fold; firstly it allows access to the forested areas so we can pick mushrooms, and secondly it provides a clear field of fire for the hunters when they come to reduce the local wild boar population - and this is becoming important because the boar are not only digging up and blocking the drainage ditches, but have also started to dig massive holes in the road between the

132

two houses. Hopefully a successful shoot means we'll be given some wild boar meat. I faithfully promise we will maintain Asterix's high standards by not boiling it and serving it with mint sauce.

Wednesday 27th
The Martin's Wallop Elderflower Champagne had finally stopped fermenting and was bottled today. This batch delivered 18 litres (24 bottles). It's our strongest brew yet, weighing in at a very respectable 17.4% ABV.

Thursday 28th
Our parcel of electrical bits and pieces arrived this afternoon. A three-day period between purchase and delivery; this must be a record for this area. The tricky thing is going to be upgrading the house wiring whilst living here. The only way I can think of achieving this is by tackling one room at a time. It would certainly have been easier if we had somewhere else to stay whilst the house was being renovated. But we looked at the prices of caravans, and have decided that putting up with a bit of inconvenience will allow the budget to be allocated to more things needing renovation.

Friday 29th
The pantry shelf assemblies have been put together and installed, and are looking quite good - at least we can now put our kitchen stuff away!

The other job I started today was the electrical renovation; I installed an earthing rod together with its connecting wire. At least now our electrical supply is properly earthed.

Wildlife diary: Mrs Jemima Puddleduck proudly reappeared, followed by seven little ducklings.

Saturday 30th

LSS did some work in the garden today, and Mrs Jemima Puddleduck took great exception to this, quacking madly. I happened to glance out of the kitchen window to see what was going on, and noticed that the quacking had attracted the attention of a large grey-brown fox which approached the fairly low fence near the back of the pond in order to investigate the source of the noise. I went into the garden, and the fox made a beeline for the woods and disappeared.

July

NEW number plates are obtained, our borehole is drilled, and we buy a trailer.

Sunday 1st

All was quiet on the pond today, so I went to see if the ducks were still in residence. On the way through the thick grass, I nearly stepped on a large snake. I grabbed the cat which had, as usual, followed me, and locked her indoors. I then went back with a spade to despatch the snake, but it had gone. Fortunately, as it happens. Further online investigation revealed that it was a non-venomous grass snake, *Natrix natrix*, and not a puff-adder or cobra as I had first thought. Well of course you don't get those in France! Anyway, there was no trace of either duck or ducklings, so we can only assume that Mr. Fox returned last night and jumped over the fence for a snack.

Monday 2nd

Now, I need to give you some background to today's discourse, which involves re-registering a foreign vehicle in France. After some research online, I found that in order to do this, you need sundry paperwork including something called a "*Quittus Fiscal*" which you obtain from your local *Hotel des Impots* (tax office). This document simply states that tax has been paid on the vehicle.

A couple of weeks ago, LSS had called the local tax office, which is the sub-prefecture in Romorantin, to ask when she could pay them a visit in order to get a *Quittus Fiscal*.

"What are your opening hours? I'd like to obtain a *Quittus Fiscal*," she explained.

"A quitty what?" they asked.

"A *Quittus Fiscal*. I've brought my vehicle to France from the UK and I need to re-register it on a French number plate."

"Oh, that sort of *Quittus Fiscal*. No, you don't need one of those, unless you bought the vehicle specifically to import it to France."

"No, I've had the car for 8 years," LSS said.

"Oh, that's fine then. It falls under your personal property so you don't need a *Quittus Fiscal* for that."

I suggested that LSS check this information. According to a fairly recent article I'd found online, we needed one. So she called the Head Honcho department itself, the *Prefecture* in Blois.

"Please can you confirm whether or not I need a *Quittus Fiscal* in order to re-register my English car in France?" she asked.

"No, you don't need a *Quittus Fiscal* any more," was the reply.

Bon. So this morning off we went to the *Prefecture* in Blois to get the *Carte Grise* for the Hyundai. It's only 60km away but it's an hour's drive, because the roads are all "D" roads (D means Departmental. Although generally in good condition, there are lots of twists and turns, and speeds are lower).

After joining a fairly short queue, we reached the counter in the *Prefecture* dealing with car registrations.

136

"Car documents?" queried the clerk behind the counter when LSS explained she wanted a *Carte Grise* for an English car. The registration document (V5) was handed over.

"Stamp!" went the rubber stamp.

"*Bon*. Request for car re-registration?"

This was handed over too (can you see where this is going?)

"Stamp!" went the rubber stamp.

"*Bon. Certificate de Conformité?*"

This joined the growing pile. "Stamp!" went the rubber stamp, again.

"*Bon. Quittus Fiscal?*"

(Pregnant pause).

"Er, what? This is no longer required. I specifically called to ask if I needed one and your offices here confirmed that I didn't," LSS exclaimed.

"Oh no," the clerk replied. "I don't know who you spoke to, but you need one."

Steam started rising from the top of LSS's head at this point.

"So I've got to go all the way back to Romorantin to get a document which your offices here told me I didn't need?" LSS asked sweetly.

I took cover behind a potted plant to avoid being splattered by the clerk's blood, as I was sure that she was about to be dragged over the counter by the hair and beaten to death with the life-sized marble bust of Marie Antoinette which graced her desk (with the inscription "The people don't have any bread!" "Hah. Let them eat their *Quittus Fiscals*.")

"No," the clerk replied. "You can go to the local *Hotel des Impots* here to get one. Go out of the building, turn left, and it's just past the shops."

I followed in LSS's wake, dodging the clouds of steam.

"Bloody country! Who in their right minds would want to be French!" she declaimed loudly (in French) to the queue of hopefuls waiting in line to get their own vehicle documents.

Of course we couldn't find the place straight away, so we had to pop into a local coffee shop to ask directions to the *Hotel des Impots.* The helpful owner directed us to the wrong building, but we eventually found the right place and informed the receptionist that we required a *Quittus Fiscal.* We were asked to take a seat whilst the correct employee was found.

Unfortunately when this employee arrived, we were informed that Blois could not give us a *Quittus Fiscal* after all; it had to be issued by the local offices in Romorantin.

The drive home was completed in total silence. We had lunch, then drove the 37km to Romorantin where we marched into their *Hotel des Impots* and asked for a *Quittus Fiscal.* We were told to take a seat, and shortly thereafter a portly bearded man asked us for the vehicle documents (I'd brought the ST1100 documents as well, just in case, although I was still waiting for its *Certificate de Conformité*).

The *Quittus Fiscal* document was filled out within minutes, and handed over to us as easy as you like. So tomorrow we need to go BACK to Blois, this time with all the documents they want. I just hope it's a different clerk this time. The good thing is that now I have the *Quittus Fiscal* for the bike too, so as soon as the *Certificate de Conformité* turns up I can once again visit Blois.

France is definitely a nation of paper-pushers. I've noticed that every desk has its own photocopy machine.

Tuesday 3rd

Our return to Blois was fairly uneventful. It was actually the same cashier we saw yesterday; I was expecting her to complain that the date stamp on the documents was now incorrect, but no. We handed over the paperwork (including the infamous *Quittus Fiscal!*) and were rewarded by being instructed to go to the cashier to pay €211 (€6 for the paperwork, and €205 for Regional Taxes). Still, I suppose we shouldn't complain; there are currently no annual road taxes in France, unlike in Britain, and the *Contrôle Technique* (MOT in Britain, or in other words a roadworthiness certificate) only needs to be done every two years, not annually as in Britain. Speaking of MOT's, here there are specific centres that do these. That is all they do, so unlike garages in Britain which offer an MOT service, there's no incentive to find things wrong so you can be charged an arm and a leg to fix them. (I'm not saying that all UK MOT garages are like this, but the last one we went to in Reading told us that the lights were not working, which was really strange as I had checked them all myself just before driving to the MOT test.) Draw your own conclusions.

On the way home, with LSS happily clutching her temporary *Carte Grise*, we stopped and had three new number plates made (one extra for the future trailer).

I spent the afternoon cutting up some fallen branches at the aged FIL's house, whilst LSS drove the tractor around, cutting more grass. Oh yes, and I also received a parcel today; the 1500W rotary hammer which I had purchased from an Ebay seller in Belgium on Sunday. Now that's what I call rapid service. It was not only cheaper to buy it from Belgium, but quicker to get than buying it locally (they would have had to order it). Now installing the next windows should be a lot easier.

Wildlife diary: The heron returned to the pond this evening, and after stalking up and down for a few minutes, pounced. We watched it catch a carp about 20cm long. It flew off into the adjacent field to enjoy its dinner. (The heron, not the carp. The carp *was* dinner).

Friday 6th

We received a telephone call regarding the borehole; they will be here on Monday to carry out the preparatory work. Because we were considered a priority case (lacking a supply of potable water qualified us as such) we have only had to wait two months for this. I hate to think how long we would have had to wait if we weren't a priority!

Sunday 8th

We went to the equestrian show in Lamotte Beuvron in the afternoon. It's a lot larger than we thought; because it hosts the French National championships there were thousands of people attending. However, we were nearly flattened several times. Not by horses, as you would think, but by bicycles. There were thousands of those too.

Monday 9th

Today the borehole chappie's son turned up to do some preparatory work. This involved digging three huge holes with a digger. A total of ten cubic metres of earth was removed. It doesn't sound like much, but believe me these holes are big! They are to contain the mud/water reserve for the drilling process. Apparently the team will arrive on Thursday to drill the borehole itself.

Tuesday 10th

Pixie our cat didn't turn up for breakfast. For her, this was highly unusual, as her most common question appears to be "Ooh, something new. Can I eat it?" We found her in the "loft" above the workshop. Later in the morning she still hadn't had breakfast, and she had by now curled up in the grass near the impending borehole. Something wasn't right, and when we finally managed to coax her over, we found that her right eye was shut, and the eyeball was bloody. There had obviously been some sort of incident last night and something like a thorn or pine needle had punctured her eye. So we shot off to the vet in Salbris.

I was very impressed; although we didn't have an appointment we were seen straight away. It doesn't appear to be too serious an injury; she had some injections and we have two lots of drops to put in her eye at least ten times a day. So she's been confined to the house for the next couple of days at least so we can keep an eye on her (in more ways than one). The vet bill seemed quite reasonable - it would appear veterinary treatment in France is a great deal cheaper than it is in Britain.

Wednesday 11th

After a visit to the bank, the car is now fully insured through *Crédit Agricole*. After much negotiating, LSS ended up with a fairly good deal - including roadside assistance - for roughly the same price as the previous UK insurance. So in the afternoon I fitted the new French number plates; the car looks very strange with these! We're still putting the eye drops in the cat's eye every hour or so; the eye itself is improving in appearance but is still half full of blood. It gives her a very evil look!

Thursday 12th

By lunchtime, the borehole drillers still hadn't turned up, so LSS called them.

"Oh, sorry, there's been a delay," said the office staff member. "Didn't the foreman call you?"

"No."

"Oh, the naughty man. Isn't he a scamp! Well, we'll try and pencil it in for Monday next week."

Not that there's any rush, of course. The one thing we have a surfeit of at the moment, is water. You may have noticed that it's been a while since I've mentioned the weather. This is not to say that we've been having marvellous sunshine; it's simply that the rain has become so commonplace that I don't even mention it any more. I think since we've been in France we've had one whole week without rain. The rest of the time it's just damp. Or windy. Or damp and windy.

LSS has been struggling with the garden, as the potatoes now have mildew, and the tomatoes are starting to look sickly as well. She's sprayed everything with Bordeaux mixture, but even this is having limited effect because no sooner are the plants sprayed, than it starts raining again and everything gets washed off. Mind you, this stuff is meant to be more of a preventative measure than a cure, so the plants were probably sprayed too late for it to be of any use.

Tuesday 17th

We finally have a borehole! The drillers turned up yesterday lunchtime with their drilling machine, and made a start, knocking off just before 6 p.m. This morning at 9 a.m. they were back on the job, and by lunchtime it was complete. They hit a small amount of water at 5m (that's the depth of the well), found a slightly greater flow at 24m, but kept going. At 35m depth they encountered a good flow of water, and carried on drilling until it stopped at 49m. Once they'd put the plastic liner into the hole and filled the outside with sand, the water level had settled; they recommended that the borehole pump be installed at a depth of 40m.

Oh yes - and the tow bar for the Hyundai finally arrived today. It was purchased online (from a French company) on the 22nd June. When we ordered and paid for it, we were assured it was in stock. Just imagine how long it would have taken to get here if it hadn't been in stock! This is by no means the first example of slack customer service we've received, so we have decided to avoid buying anything else from France or French companies if it can at all be avoided. It's also more expensive.

Other European countries fare better on the customer service front. I bought an SDS+ rotary hammer drill from a company in Belgium; it arrived within two days. On Saturday

LSS had contacted three companies for a quote for a second-hand shipping container. We thought this could be a useful item to have, as it would enable us to empty the barn of all our stored boxes and furniture so that we could then lay a proper floor. One of the companies was Austrian, but unfortunately stated that the enquiry would be passed on to their local (French) agent. On each of these companies' websites, a rapid response to any enquiries was promised.

So, Dear Reader, how many of these companies do you think has responded with an actual quote? Or even an email to say they aren't going to bother? If you said "Zero", have a banana.

Saturday 21st

Having received our tow bar, I did indeed have to dismantle the rear of the Hyundai in order to install it. I also had to employ my soldering iron in order to splice the tow bar electrical socket into the vehicle's wiring loom.

But I'm pleased to report that not only does the car have a tow bar, we now have a trailer as well! We had been on the lookout for one for a while now, but the lowest price found to date was just over €650. The thing is, with us being in the middle of nowhere, the only viable way for us to purchase DIY materials is with the aid of a trailer. Delivery charges are just ridiculous. Yesterday LSS was once again looking on the Internet for trailers. Lo and behold, Castorama had a special offer. They were selling exactly the type of trailer we were looking for, priced at €499, with a jockey wheel and tarpaulin included. So this morning we were up early and headed for Orleans.

And there they were. A long row of nice, shiny, DIY-material-carrying, galvanized steel trailers, just outside the main entrance.

After a fair bit of running around (none of the staff at Castorama seemed to be sure that they actually sold trailers, where they would be stocked if they did indeed sell trailers, or at which particular cashier payment should be made), we finally ended up with one chap who dealt with the transaction. He was a bit condescending initially; but once I'd demonstrated that I knew how to work a trailer hitch and connect the electrical plug, he mellowed a bit.

He said he'd had one customer who took fifteen minutes before he was able to connect the trailer hitch to the tow bar. And when he drove off, the trailer remained behind as he'd still not connected the hitch correctly.

I'd brought some duct tape with which to temporarily attach the number plate to the trailer, but the helpful chap from Castorama waved it away, whipped out some double-sided tape and proceeded to fix the number plate himself. I should have known better. When we arrived home, the number plate was missing. I suspect it dropped off as soon as we exited the Castorama car park. So now on Monday we need to go and have yet another number plate made.

Interlude

-§§§-

Diary entries became more sporadic from this point onwards. It was not due to the lack of anything noteworthy occurring; but I became increasingly busy. For example, the old wooden box on the lounge wall which previously held three old ceramic fuses was replaced with a new electricity switch panel with fourteen separate circuit breakers.

-§§§-

August

S OME wild boar pay us a visit, our composting toilet is installed, and we take a very long unplanned stroll next to the Loire river.

Thursday 9th
We did get another number plate made up for the trailer, and I riveted it in place as required by French law. The trailer was then put to immediate use; we went to BricoDepot near Bourges and bought three more PVC double-glazed windows, a PVC double-glazed front door, and a wooden door. The wooden door is for the kitchen; the problem is that the existing door is not a standard size. It's narrow, and fairly short. (Actually none of the door and window openings here are standard. Well, I suppose they may have been standard in eighteen-fifty-something when the house was built, but that doesn't help when buying modern doors or windows!)

Modification of the window openings is possible, and the front door opening can be widened. But as far as the kitchen door is concerned, rather than chopping out the lintel and installing a new one, I've calculated that the easiest solution is to cut a piece off the bottom of a new door. And it's easier to do this type of operation on a wooden door rather than one made of PVC. So I've made a start with that - at least the radial arm saw is once again proving its worth!

However, some work will need to be done on the door opening as well. The new wooden door is wider; so some chiselling of the surrounding brickwork needs to be carried out. I knew that SDS+ rotary hammer would come in handy!

We've also ordered an Italian-made borehole pump from Belgium, a Swedish dry toilet from Germany, and a Chinese-made wood-burning boiler stove from Britain. These items should arrive next week.

Concerning the dry toilet, we had decided we would only order this once we had completed the installation of a proper floor in the attached barn. Well, next to the outbuilding now being used as a workshop is another small building, divided into two rooms by a brick wall. This had originally housed pigs. One room has been used for scrap metal storage; whenever we find something old and rusty we just toss it through the large gap above the rotted door. Once the room is full, we will take it all to a scrap metal dealer and get some cash for it. The other room has a door in slightly better condition, and a small slot serving as a window. I had previously only peered in through the slot, but had never actually entered the room. All that could be seen in the gloom was a rotten plastic chair and some barbed wire on reels. Well, a couple of days ago I decided to add the barbed wire to the scrap metal pile, so prised open the wooden door and went inside. Immediately I was cursing, because I'd banged my head rather hard on the lintel. The doorway is only about four feet high.

Mopping at the wound with my handkerchief, I went inside again, this time bent double. I proceeded to clear the room of rubbish. Then I made The Discovery!

No, not a pot of gold under the two ceramic toilet bowls resting in one corner. That would have been nice. But the room has a concrete floor! It is in fact the best floor in the entire building complex. So this will be the room in which the dry toilet can be installed, until such time as we have a proper bathroom in the barn. No more wearing raincoats when we need to visit the lavatory!

Unfortunately I had to kill a viper two days ago. The cat was displaying her usual interest in something moving, asking her usual question "Oooh, it moves. Can I eat it?" Fortunately LSS saw the situation developing. The cat was rapidly removed to the kitchen whilst I dealt with the snake. I didn't like despatching it - after all, they are useful in keeping down the population of rodents etc. but we just can't take any chances with the cat. She already has a damaged eye from (we presume) a bramble thorn after having been (we presume) chased by a fox. She's now fully recovered but one of her pupils does not close as much as the other, and the iris is a slightly darker colour, so she looks a bit like David Bowie.

As the kitchen has now been re-wired, we now have our freezer installed so have been able to have some ice cream!

The aged FIL's washing machine finally stopped working altogether last week, so acting upon his instructions, LSS telephoned his customary white goods supplier in a nearby village. This week the supplier delivered and installed a new washing machine and removed the old one. For a price, of course.

Saturday 11th
We have now met our closest permanent neighbours, so here's another abbreviation for you. They're a very pleasant

couple we shall call T&M. T visited us with one of his neighbours, who had been asked to look after a dog for a friend who was going to Paris for a week. Well, he didn't do a very good job, because the dog escaped. So he and T were visiting all the neighbouring properties to ask if anyone had seen it. (The dog was later found in a nearby village, having crossed a very busy main road. Due to the microchip with which it was implanted, the vet telephoned the owner. Who was very surprised, considering they had left it under the – ahem - watchful eye of a friend of theirs.)

I think T also took this as an opportunity to find out a bit more about us. They had been living in the neighbourhood for approximately five years, and had frequently taken countryside walks, their route often taking them past this neglected property. Until last year they had even once or twice passed the time of day with the aged FIL, if he had happened to be pottering around the garden when they went past.

T had remarked to M that it was an ideal little place, and if it was ever advertised for sale, he'd be first in line. Soon after we'd moved in, he happened to go past on his way back from the village bakery; and must have noticed our car's UK registration plates. He immediately sped home to tell M, and she later told us about this.

"I can't believe it!" he had exclaimed. "That property – the one we like – it's been sold! I've missed out! And I didn't see it advertised for sale anywhere! But that's not the worst part. The new people - they're *Anglais!*"

Of course, having found out that the property had not, in fact, been sold; and that LSS was the daughter of the owner, he mellowed considerably. And he is now taking the opportunity of practising his English whilst teaching me the French words for sundry DIY items.

Sunday 12th

We visited neighbour J, as she had telephoned yesterday to let us know the elderberries were ready for picking! We took a large bucket and filled it with berries, so today this year's batch of elderberry wine is on the go.

The elder (*Sambucus nigra*) is a marvellous tree as far as we're concerned. In spring it provides elderflower cordial and elderflower champagne; and later in the year when the berries are ripe, one can make elderberry cordial and elderberry wine. The elderberry cordial is of particular benefit as a cough syrup, and being particularly high in Vitamin C enables one to ward off any winter sniffles. The elderberry wine is marvellous too; we've yet to be disappointed with a batch. Be warned though, raw berries can be toxic.

Elderberry Wine Recipe:

(Hydrometer required)

Ingredients:

400g berries per litre of water

Sugar

Wine yeast

1 tsp yeast nutrient per 4.5 litres

1 Vitamin B tablet per 4.5 litres

1 tsp citric acid per 4.5 litres

1 tsp pectolase per 4.5 litres

Method:

Cover fruit with water, add citric acid, and bring to the boil.

Remove from heat, and take a sample of the liquid. Allow sample to cool to room temperature.

Using hydrometer, measure the initial density and then add enough sugar to result in a final alcohol content of around 14%ABV.

Stir well, reheating if necessary, until the sugar has melted.

Allow to cool to room temperature and place in fermentation vessel.

Add yeast, vitamin B tablets, and yeast nutrient.

Cover loosely and leave until aerobic fermentation stops.

Strain and squeeze the pulp to extract as much liquid as possible.

Add pectolase.

Rack into demi-johns and fit airlock.

When secondary fermentation ceases, rack into clean demi-johns and leave for a week for sedimentation to settle.

Rack again, measure final density, and add 1 Campden tablet per 4.5 litres of wine.

Bottle.

Keep for at least a year before drinking.

Monday 13th

Today we received the borehole pump we ordered from Belgium. Not only did we receive it on the day we were promised; but it was actually hand-delivered by the Area Sales Manager (Benelux) with whom I had corresponded regarding the order. This was outstanding customer service. Granted, he was going to be in the vicinity anyway, as he was visiting family in the area, but it's still amazing. We were in complete shock for the rest of the day.

I also booked an airline ticket to South Africa to visit my aged mother (who is 92 this year). Unfortunately we can't both afford to go, so LSS will have to soldier on without me for a week.

The rest of the day was spent working on shortening the new kitchen door which we bought. The door opening measures 194.5cm in height but the door is 220cm high. I managed to dismantle the bottom section using the radial arm saw and the router, and having cut the door (and of course frame) to the required height I am now in the process of reassembling the bottom rails and weather-strip.

The cat has gone missing. Again. She does tend to treat this place like a McDonald's drive-through, but this is becoming ridiculous. She didn't turn up for dinner last night, but first thing this morning we noticed her food bowl was empty, so she must have come home during the night. We have an electronic cat flap which is programmed to unlock when it reads her microchip, so no other animal could have eaten her dinner. The cat flap will of course be installed in the new door. These devices don't seem to exist around here; visitors to the house are always amazed by it.

Wildlife diary: Yesterday morning LSS was in the garden, weeding the green beans, and I was catching up with my electronic correspondence. I looked up to see her making faces at me through the window and pointing towards the road. I went out to see what was going on, and as I opened the door

she made hushing gestures (the finger-to-the-lips type thing).
Then I heard it.

"Oink, oink". "Snort, snort". "Oink, oink, snort".

I moved cautiously to the property entrance and not ten
metres away was a family of ten wild boar. I don't know if
they saw us or not but they trotted off down the lane, and
turned off into one of our fields. Well, I say "fields"; they're
more like "forested areas" now. Not long after that, boar
number eleven trotted out from behind a chestnut tree where
he had been hiding, and he proceeded to try and catch up
with the family group. My first encounter with the elusive
Sus scrofa scrofa. Obelix would have loved it. (These animals
can be dangerous though, so one needs to be careful).

Thursday 16th

Today I have three virtual Customer Service medals to
award. Let me explain.

On the 7th August we ordered three large items:

1. A Separett composting toilet from a company in Germany. Why Germany? Well, their prices were at the
   SRP (suggested retail price) levels, and delivery was free.
   If we had ordered it from the French distributor, prices
   were higher and delivery was extra. And delivery would
   take four months. Yes, you read that correctly. Four
   months. The toilet itself is made in Sweden.

2. A wood burning stove with integrated back boiler from
   England. Why England? (Spain was the other alternative). The prices were the lowest, the selection of stoves
   was larger, and France was not an option anyway; we

could not find a French company selling boiler stoves. The attitude seemed to be "Why would you want a stove to heat water? That's what electricity is for, *n'est ce pas?*"

3. A ZDS borehole pump from a company in Belgium. Why Belgium? Well, once again I didn't want to order anything from a French distributor. As it's now August, most French staff are on holiday. The reason I chose this Italian-made borehole pump is that it has an innovative integrated pump protector which eliminates the need for a control panel.

The above items were all paid for on the same day, Tuesday 7th August. Delivery for all of them was promised for the week commencing 13th August.

The bronze medal goes to:

Germany. The composting toilet arrived today. (I installed it this afternoon in the outbuilding with the recently-discovered concrete floor). We're both delighted with it as this means that we don't have to apply mosquito repellent to our bottoms any more. And did you know mosquito repellent does not repel horseflies? Don't ask how we know.

Second place, and the silver medal goes to:

The United Kingdom. The stove arrived yesterday. Weighing in at a hefty 130kg, it has not been installed yet, but we managed to move it into the lounge with the aid of two trestles, a wooden beam, some nylon rope, and my hand trolley.

But first place, and the gold medal, goes to:

Belgium. Not only was the pump delivered on Monday this week (its scheduled delivery day), but it was hand-delivered by the Benelux area Sales Manager himself.

Sunday 19th

Today we went to visit Friend L in Bonny-sur-Loire. Her latest hand-built kayak was examined and admired. After lunch, she suggested a short stroll to have a look at the Loire river.

"Why not?" we said. Silly us.

Is there a canicule (heat wave) warning broadcast on the radio? Check.

Temperature outside 43 degrees Centigrade? Check.

One bottle of 1.5 litres water for three people? Check.

Fifteen kilometres and three and a half hours later....

LSS has blisters on her toes from not wearing proper walking shoes. If we'd known we were going to do a fifteen kilometer walk we would have been more properly dressed! Other than that we're fine, so we must be a lot fitter than we thought. Mind you, we did see some fish in the river from the vantage point of one of the bridges. They appeared to be salmon, and must have been nearly a metre in length. We also bumped into a retired English couple in their campervan and stopped for a chat.

Friday 24th

The kitchen door installation has now been completed. I finished the rendering of the brickwork surrounding the frame this morning. In the afternoon we went to the aged FIL's house to fetch the washing which LSS had put in the machine earlier. I stuck my head in the kitchen door to say hello.

After saying hello back, "*Mouton*," the aged FIL mumbled.

My brain flicked rapidly through its dictionary section, finding the index cards for the letter M. "Um, sorry, I don't think this is going to help," it told me. "According to my records, *Mouton* is mutton, or a sheep. So why the aged FIL is saying 'mutton' to you does not compute. To quote Spock, 'It's not logical.' So I'm afraid you're on your own."

I must have looked rather blank, because the aged FIL repeated it again. "*Mouton*," he said. I could see him thinking "Why didn't my daughter marry a nice French bloke instead, then I wouldn't have all this trouble."

"Er, I'm sorry, I don't understand," I said in French, and hurried out to the washing line where LSS had just about finished removing the dried laundry.

"*Mouton* is French for 'mutton', isn't it?" I asked.

"Yes, why?" she answered.

"Because that's what your father just said to me."

Her eyebrows shot upwards. We re-entered the kitchen and she asked him to repeat what he'd said to me. He did.

"Ah!" LSS chuckled. "He said, '*beau temps*' (nice weather). Not '*mouton*'".

Oh dear...

September

O<small>N</small> my returnfrom South Africa, I discover a theft of expensive tools from the aged FIL, and we find rats in the well.

Friday 14th

This entry could be titled "How to steal from the Elderly; they make easy targets".

I've been back at La Darnoire for a week, following my trip to South Africa to see my mother. She's unfortunately not in the best of health, and suffers from dementia at times. She's in the "frail care" section of a care home. At first she didn't recognise me. She then thought I was – in sequence - my sister's boyfriend, my sister's husband, and then my father, finally coming to the realisation of who I actually was. Still, she is 92 this year so it's excusable!

However, quite a few of my mother's things have been stolen since she's been in the care home, including her gold wristwatch that she'd had for decades. Anything nice which my sister brings her disappears as well; sadly even things like hand cream. I suppose there's some consolation in the fact that Mum doesn't realise things have gone missing. But I don't want you to get the impression that thefts like this only happen in South Africa. Whilst I was away, there was a theft from the aged FIL's workshop here by one of the carers. The carer was male (the only male in the bunch) and knowing that I'd be away, he had asked the aged FIL if he had some welding goggles he could borrow.

Stupidly the aged FIL gave him the key to the workshop padlock so that he could go and look. The carer then "forgot" to replace the key in its usual place, and the following day said that he had "lost" it (so we think he came back that night). The day after that, as soon as she found out that the key had gone missing, LSS became suspicious and went into the workshop to investigate - having first searched for and found a duplicate key, of course. The chaotic mess in the workshop still resembled a chaotic mess. The locked cash box which the aged FIL kept in the workshop under a pile of empty plastic chainsaw oil containers was untouched. (The cash box is now no longer kept in the workshop). LSS then changed the padlock on the workshop door.

It was only last Sunday that I had a chance to visit the workshop to see if I could determine whether anything was missing from amongst the piles of tools. Unfortunately something *was* missing, probably the most expensive piece of equipment there. A petrol-powered Stihl branch trimming chainsaw, priced at around €800.

The aged FIL was unaware of the theft and we couldn't tell him because it would, quite literally, make him ill. We can't tell the police either, because the theft happened two weeks ago. And we also can't claim on the house insurance because the aged FIL had stupidly given the thief the key to the door! On a positive note, that particular carer is not looking after the aged FIL any more (he handed in his notice on that Friday - I wonder why!)

Anyway, that's enough negative news. On the day after my return from South Africa I received a document from

Honda Paris saying my motorcycle is actually road legal to use in France, so yesterday we went to the *Prefecture* in Blois, and after paying them just over €100, I was issued with a temporary *Carte Grise*. Next on the agenda is a new number plate, and then I commence battle with sundry insurance companies. Once the vehicle insurance is sorted out we can take the bike out on the road again for the first time in months.

During the past week I have installed an electricity supply to the loft. This is where I will be installing the water pressure vessel with pressure switch. At the same time I wired in an overhead fluorescent light. Finally we can see what we're doing without needing a torch or having to plug in a long extension lead! Next week I intend to continue the double-glazing installation, so hopefully by wintertime we'll be fully insulated!

Sunday 16th

This morning LSS and I visited some of the bramble patches which exist all over the property. After two hours or so of picking blackberries, we had just over 4kg. These will be used to make our first-ever batch of blackberry wine. I just need to wait for our home-brewed beer to finish fermenting, and then I can start the wine-making process.

I also took the opportunity of getting rid of some of the large pile of twigs and smaller branches, burning them in the brazier. This was not wasted fuel; I made some more charcoal at the same time. Yesterday I spent the afternoon with the chainsaw, cutting up one of the fallen branches from a large oak tree at the aged FIL's house. There's certainly enough wood there for the winter! And I also need to cut up another entire tree when I have some spare time. It was blown over by the tornado we had earlier in the year. The base of the trunk must be over a metre in diameter.

This afternoon I made some more bread (yes, I make my own. I have done so for years. I do use a Kenwood bread maker machine though).

We had noticed that the pump which draws water from the well had been rather slow in filling up the pressure vessel recently. I suspected that the filter on the well side of the pipe may have become clogged, so we opened the well cover to have a look. Unfortunately we discovered two drowned rats floating in the water. They'd been there a while I think, as one of them seemed to have lost all its fur. Ah-ha! That's probably what was clogging the pipes! We fished them out with a landing net (normally used for fishing). It wasn't a very nice discovery - not that we drink the well water of course. But I had thought our bath water had been starting to smell a bit funny. Before use, that is.

Monday 17th

Not much news to report today; I spent the entire day removing the old bedroom window and installing the new double-glazed replacement. I managed to retain the external frame which holds the shutters, so that's another job for LSS to do - repainting these!

Wildlife diary: A woodpecker was practising his percussion solo in the chestnut trees. I've no idea which type it was, as it was difficult to see through the leaves. I do know it wasn't a green woodpecker as it was much smaller than this species. We also saw four deer grazing in the meadow beyond the pond.

Friday 28th

"Don't bother me," said the Sergeant. Just not in so many words.

Regarding the theft from the aged FIL, further items have come to light. Or rather, they have not come to light because they're missing. As is usually the case, you only realise something has gone when you have need of it.

We're missing a steel toolbox containing a lot of spanners, and a boxed screwdriver set. Last week I needed to pump up the tractor tyres which were looking a bit flat. Lo and behold, the tyre inflator (the type you attach to a compressor) was also conspicuous by its absence.

So yesterday LSS spoke to the *Garde Champêtre* (the local town clerk/village policeman) who suggested that she make a statement to the police. It's not that we are hopeful of getting the stolen items returned, but if it helps to prevent thefts from other aged persons in future...

Off we went to the *Gendarmerie* in Salbris where the only person on duty in the entire building seemed to be the desk sergeant. LSS explained the situation. The desk sergeant then informed us that what we had to do was to telephone the thief to ask him to return the items he'd taken.

Yes, Dear Reader, that's what he said.

This advice seemed rather odd, so we slept on it. This morning, it still seemed rather odd. In my view it could open the door to all sorts of nastiness including possible defamation of character lawsuits etc. etc. But as we don't have the thief's telephone number anyway, LSS spoke to the manager of the domestic aid service (the thief's ex-employer). The manager was equally puzzled by this advice.

So LSS called the police sergeant again, to make an appointment so that she could give an official statement. The sergeant was considerably annoyed that LSS had not followed his advice.

"In my experience, this solves cases of theft," he said. I kid you not.

Wow, groundbreaking stuff! If this technique gets out, I can see the crime statistics dropping through the floor. It makes one wonder why we have a police force at all. Personally I think the desk sergeant didn't want to have to do any more work than was absolutely necessary.

We discussed the matter with the aged FIL (who is now aware of what's missing) and he just wants the whole matter dropped.

Speaking of the aged FIL, before moving to France we had initially been concerned that he would be underfoot the whole time, getting involved in the renovations. As he's a fairly difficult character, we were dreading the "Don't do it like that, do it like this" type of advice. One doesn't mind so much if the advice-giver knows his onions, but this would not have been the case.

Well, as it turned out, our fears were groundless. Not only does the aged FIL spend his days in bed, but he does not want to hear about what we're doing. LSS has tried to get him interested without success. In fact it makes him cross. She mentioned that, after moving in, we had switched off the electric fence around the garden to avoid electrocuting the cat. "You can't do that!" he exclaimed. "You'll have battalions of wild boar ploughing up your vegetables."

To date, our vegetables have remained un-ploughed. And the cat is not electrified.

We had also created an opening in the fence at the bottom of the garden. (This was temporary, I hasten to add.) The opening was to allow access for the tractor, so that the grass-cutting attachment could clear the worst of the weeds. When she inadvertently mentioned this, he became quite angry. "You're destroying all my good work," he complained.

So now we don't tell him anything.

October

N EW windows are fitted, the borehole pump is installed and tested, Cat goes missing, and we try and rid the house of mould.

Wednesday 3rd

Goodness gracious, it's October already! Doesn't time fly when you're having fun?

We've been exceedingly busy at La Darnoire Towers recently. Yesterday I bottled our home brewed 7.5% beer, and today was the turn of this year's batch of 15.3% elderberry wine. This pleasant task was unfortunately interrupted by having to cut some more wood for the wood stove. We're still working our way through all the scrap wood we put to one side when we first moved in, and I suspect there's still enough left to see us through the winter. At least we can heat our bathwater on the kitchen stove without it costing us anything!

On the home renovation front, the new double-glazed windows have now been installed in the bedroom and lounge, and the walls around the windows have been re-rendered with lime.

Today an important task was accomplished. Last Saturday LSS and I had lowered the new borehole pump into the borehole, having first of all securely attached to it a long piece of nylon rope. As one does. After all, one needs to be able to retrieve the pump again! To supply power to the pump, we re-used some rigid cables which the aged FIL had lying around. Rigid cables are not the easiest electrical wiring with which to work, but it's what we had.

The pump is situated at a depth of forty metres, and feeding the combination of rigid cable, nylon rope, and thick-walled 32mm diameter water pipe down the borehole tube was not the easiest task in the world either, as the water pipe constantly tried re-coiling itself. At times it felt like we were wrestling an octopus.

Well, today we fed the remaining 25m of water pipe through the corrugated tubing which had been buried to a depth of 80cm (for frost protection). It links the borehole itself to the house. I then jury-rigged a length of three-core cable to the borehole electric switch, and connected a garden hosepipe to the borehole pipe to lead the water away. We are pleased to report that the pump is working very well, and the sight of our own borehole water gushing out of the hosepipe led me to dance a jig. Those that know me well would agree that this was a very unusual occurrence indeed.

T&M, our neighbours in the next county (they're actually just down the road from us, but the county border lies at one edge of the property) had kindly given us an old 500-litre pressure vessel (*ballon*) which they no longer required. They had become frequent visitors, often dropping in for a chat.

We've decided to use this galvanized steel tank as our thermal store for the hot water. This will involve cutting the top off, cleaning it out thoroughly, and then drilling lots of holes for the various water pipe connections. But obviously, a cold water supply is required first, hence the excitement at getting the borehole pump working!

On the kitchen front, LSS has made several pots of tomato sauce, several jars of tomato ketchup, lots of tomato soup, stuffed tomatoes... (do you spot a trend here?)

The garden has also produced lots of courgettes, carrots, beans, peas, beetroot, turnips, and - my personal favourites - gala melons and watermelons! Not to mention the strawberries, blueberries and raspberries, of course.

Unfortunately we had to throw away our batch of blackberry wine. Because I only had one brewing belt, I had to wait for the beer to finish fermenting before I could add the yeast to the blackberry juice. And even though I had sterilized it with some campden tablets, it had started fermenting on its own and smelled rather rank. Maybe next year!

Wildlife diary: In a word, wasps. In early summer, I noticed a few wasps flying in and out of a small opening next to the chimney, and decided to leave them alone. They appear to have built their nest between the kitchen ceiling and the floor of the roof space. They haven't really bothered us, but lately one or two have started dropping in for a visit through the gap between the kitchen ceiling and the wall. I'll be glad when they die out this winter and I can fill up their entrance hole. It has however been fascinating to watch them from the safety of the kitchen window. They are the first insects stirring in the morning, even with temperatures as low as two degrees Centigrade; and they are the last insects flying about when it gets dark. They appear to work even harder than bees.

<u>Sunday 7th</u>

It was a very grey day today, so we took the opportunity to have a haircut. I cut LSS's hair, and she cut mine. This is another cost-saving example; we have a barber's-style electric trimmer, and as we both prefer short hair, it's a fairly easy job. Although I must admit, when I first cut LSS's hair, it was not without some trepidation!

We then took a stroll down one of the woodland alleyways she had cleared with the tractor on Friday, using the heavy-duty brush cutter attachment. We've nicknamed this one "Sloe Alley" because there are several heavily-laden *Prunus spinosa* trees all in a row. We had taken a bucket with us, and about forty minutes of picking resulted in 3.3kg of fruit. The next batch of sloe wine is under way...

Some other areas of the property have also been given names.

We have "Piggy Corner", so-called because the boars have excavated a mud wallow next to one of the ditches.

There is "Borehole Field" – obviously this is a field. Which contains the borehole.

"Horse Field" is another cleared patch of land opposite the house, which will be rented out to horses at a later date. At least, it will be rented out to their owners. I don't think horses are able to pay rent, because they don't have pockets. There's an annual horsey convention in one of the local towns, so consequently there's a demand for stabling during the summer months.

And last but not least, the view from our kitchen window is of a long clearing, leading all the way down to the end of the property. This is at the lowest point, and the ground is always saturated there. So we've called this "Soggy Bottom". Which is also what you'd get if you sat down for a picnic.

After lunch we visited the chestnut trees which grow opposite the house and gathered a bowlful of chestnuts. I've started peeling them in order to make chestnut flour. It's a very labour-intensive process!

For dinner we had pot-roasted pheasant (the bird was donated to us by M&O as a thank-you present for clearing the alleyways around the fields to improve hunting access for their group of hunters). This was served with fried mushrooms which we gathered yesterday afternoon. We collected a whole basketful, and LSS has cooked and frozen some for later use. They're the parasol *Macrolepiota procera* which seem to like the grassy areas which were cut short by the tractor. Dinner was very tasty indeed.

Friday 12th

Blooming cat! She had been missing for over three days, and it was very unlike her to miss a meal. The only thing we could think of was that she'd been eaten by a fox.

We had wandered all over the property but did not see as much as a whisker. LSS and I were obviously quite upset about it, and had resigned ourselves to not seeing her again. We'd even packed away her kitty-food bowls and litter tray.

But this evening, lo and behold, she turns up, asking for dinner. No sooner had she wolfed it down, when she was off out again. I don't think we have a cat anymore. We just happen to feed one.

We later suspected she had visited a neighbouring farm and had become locked in an outbuilding accidentally. The farm is uninhabited except for weekends, and has been turned into a *gîte* (Self-catering accomodation). The owner's father pops in once or twice each week to do some maintenance work.

Wednesday 24th

Some progress has been made since my last diary entry; the double-glazed front door has finally been installed. I've also fabricated a panel to go above the door using some scrap pieces of oak; it contains two adjustable vents so at least we'll be able to regulate the airflow. Unlike the previous panel, which had an unregulated airflow because one of the panes of glass had a massive hole in it.

The continually-growing mould in the house finally became too much, so I've installed a ventilation system upstairs. It consists of an air vent in the pantry, and two in the bedroom ceiling. These are linked by means of flexible pipes to an extractor fan, which runs continually. Only time will tell whether this cures the mould or not, but at least we're now getting some extra ventilation to these rooms.

Yesterday was LSS's birthday, so we decided to celebrate by going to a restaurant. Oh dear, finding a restaurant open on a Tuesday in France is not an easy task. We drove around for ages, starting in the closest large town, Lamotte Beuvron. Every. Single. Restaurant. was closed. We ended up going to a grill in Salbris, the *"Au Coin du Feu"*, where we were the sole customers. Very nice it was too. It would appear that the French don't eat out on Tuesdays. As my birthday is on the same day of the week as LSS, it looks like we'll be going back there next month.

Work on the workshop outbuilding is also progressing nicely; I've run plastic conduit through the roof space in the barn into the workshop, and the next job is to feed the electrical wiring through the conduit. Once that is done, I'll be installing an overhead fluorescent light and a couple of plug sockets. Power tools will soon be available without having to use a 30-metre extension lead!

I also used up our stock of old car tyres in the pond. Two of the banks are eroding, and if we didn't do anything the pond would soon encompass the garden. I'd known about using tyres as erosion control, but I hadn't made the connection between the enlarging pond and erosion; it was my sister who suggested the idea whilst I was staying with her in South Africa. The local agricultural garage is only too happy to give us their old tyres (as they can't normally get rid of them without paying a hefty fee).

The garage has also turned out to be a useful source of old wooden pallets. We'll need to visit them again shortly to get some more; I'm using these to construct a wood shed. The base and lower walls have been completed - I just need to get another nine pallets to finish the walls. The roof will consist of corrugated iron - there are sundry sheets of the stuff lying around on the farm.

I must end by mentioning the wild boar hunt which took place on the property last weekend - the hunters ended up bagging two, one of which weighed in at a hefty 110kg. We went to see them butchered at a neighbouring farm, and LSS was presented with both boar heads. Undeterred, she made brawn out of them (I don't particularly like brawn, but there was sufficient meat in the neck area to make several stews. That I *do* like!)

November

E VENINGS are spent with chestnuts. I discover a Second
World War Jerry-can, and we fetch a new second-hand
kitchen range.

Monday 12th

I have a certain sympathy for our ancestors; the ones who
lived off the land. I've spent the evenings of the past two weeks
peeling chestnuts and drying them in the warming drawer of
the wood stove. I've also been shelling hazelnuts. Goodness
gracious what a lot of work. I did use some of the chestnut
flour to make some bread. It was very tasty, but the loaf
doesn't rise quite as much. The poor food processor was
struggling to make the flour; dried chestnuts are incredibly
hard. I'm considering looking for a hollow log and using it the
way that African women grind their corn. In fact that may
not be a bad idea at all.

It's been a bit chilly recently, but we're still enjoying
watermelons, cape gooseberries, raspberries; and, of course,
chestnuts. The sloe wine finally finished fermenting, so has
been bottled and put away. It's a 13.5% brew.

LSS found several pots of honey in the aged FIL's pantry;
they had been there for years. Instead of throwing them
away, we decided to make mead out of them; so we now have
a demijohn of mead bubbling away behind the fridge. We
haven't been lazy!

I also swept the chimney a couple of weeks ago, as the
stove has been smoking heavily lately. I had to do it first

thing in the morning when it was still below 2 degrees outside; the chimney-cleaning hatch is right next to a wasps nest, and the only way I could sweep the chimney without getting dive-bombed by lots of angry wasps was by doing it when it was too cold for them to fly. It took ages for my fingers to warm up afterwards. But at least we now have a clean chimney. Is there a market for around two kilograms of soot? I left it in a neat little pile in the field across the road. I know it can be used as toothpaste, but as far as recycling goes, we're drawing the line there.

We also bought some more farm diesel for the tractor recently, and in a dark recess of the fuel store at the other farmhouse I discovered a Jerry can. It's the real McCoy, the one which gave these canisters their name. It's marked *"Kraftstoff 20 l - Feuergefährlich - 1942 - Nowack Bautzen - Wehrmacht"*. It was most probably left behind by the retreating German army. Made in 1942 and still being used!

Sunday 25th

I'm pleased to report our new kitchen woodstove is working brilliantly.

"What? Another new stove?" I hear you cry. No. It's new to us, but it's second-hand, and was probably made in the 1970's. It has seen very little use though. Our old *Rosieres* was just getting more and more difficult to use, because the seals around the top cast-iron plate had long ago ceased to exist. Despite having thoroughly cleaned the chimney, we found that the only way we could get the stove going in the mornings was to open all the doors and windows, switch off the newly-installed VMC (extractor fan), and wait for half an hour before the stovepipe was hot enough to draw properly. If we missed out just one of these steps, the kitchen filled with smoke.

So last week LSS had a look on a French website for second-hand items, and we spotted a very reasonably-priced kitchen range for sale in a village about 60km away. We asked our neighbour T to help with loading and unloading, as these things must weigh nearly 200kg. As it turned out, he was very pleased we had asked him to come along to assist, because the person selling the stove also had a small forge for sale, which was just what our neighbour had been looking for! There was sufficient room on the trailer for the forge as well, so everyone was happy.

Not only that, but the stove we bought also came with a stainless steel stovepipe. Our old one was definitely not stainless steel, as it was rusty. Both stove and rusty stovepipe have now been consigned to the scrap-metal junk-pile. The new stove is installed and functioning, and not a wisp of smoke escapes when we light it! It seems to put out a lot more heat than the old one, and the dinner LSS made yesterday (burgers and potato wedges) seemed to taste even better than before.

Some progress has also been made with the household water supply. I have become a dab hand at soldering copper pipes together (it's called 'sweating', no idea why), and water has now reached our new *"ballon"* in the loft. Hopefully by the end of next week we'll have nice, clean, transparent borehole water on tap in the kitchen, which will make a nice change from the rust-coloured mouse-flavoured well water we've been using in the bath for the past seven months.

December

V ERY slow service from a French Insurance Company. Our
bread machine expires, and we have the first snow of the
winter. We finally have clean water from a tap, and we have
an interesting experience with some Romanians.

Saturday 1st
Finally! I'm able to ride my motorcycle legally in France!
The entire process from start to finish has taken seven months.
(And according to published legislation, you officially have
one month to re-register your foreign vehicle. Good luck with
that).

Of course, now that winter has arrived, I can't actually
ride anywhere anyway. It's not that I mind the weather, but
in order to get the bike to a tarmac surface one needs to
negotiate a farm track with slippery wet grass and mud for
400 metres.

So, here's what happened after I received the *Carte Grise*
in mid-September:

I contacted an insurance company called "Agence Eaton".
Why? Because this agency offers to "translate" the UK NCB
(no claims bonus) into the French equivalent (called a *"Bonus
Malus"*), which works in a completely different manner. Having
approached other insurance companies, I discovered that each
one wanted documented proof of my existing French *"Bonus
Malus"*. Stating that I did not have one of these immediately
put me into the highest insurance risk bracket, with annual
premiums approaching or even exceeding €1,000. Comparing

that with the annual £98 I was paying in the UK left me feeling very slightly annoyed.

So, on the 5th October, I accepted the quote from Agence Eaton for an annual insurance policy, at around €300. However, I had to exclude fire and theft from the policy because my ST1100 does not have every single part marked with a French-recognised identification system. Each part IS marked, but it's with a UK-based Thatcham-approved Honda Smartwater tag. And that isn't good enough for French insurers, apparently.

On the 12th October, I received the Insurance disc in the post. Oh dear. It was only valid for a month, expiring on the 9th November. LSS called the agency to ask why it was only valid for a month when I'd paid for an entire year, and was told that this was just a temporary certificate. Not to worry, the proper one would be sent to us within a week, they promised.

It was only on the 12th November (three days after the expiry of the temporary certificate) that I realised I had not yet received the full annual certificate. LSS once again called Agence Eaton, and was told that they were about to post it, and that we would receive it the following week.

19th November: Still no certificate. LSS called Agence Eaton again. She was informed that it had been posted by second class mail, and we would receive it the following week.

27th November: Still no certificate. LSS called Agence Eaton yet again – this time knowing the number by heart. This time she was told that the Agency had not yet received the certificate from the insurers, but it would be with us the following week.

Today, 1st December: The annual, full, correct certificate arrived in the post.

The thing is, if you're in the UK and you want to change insurers, you simply don't renew with your existing insurer. You just inform them, and sign up with a new one. It's all very seamless in my experience. It doesn't work like that here. Two months before your insurance policy is due to expire, you need to send the insurers a registered letter telling them you will be cancelling your policy on the expiry date. Only then can you start getting prices from other insurance companies.

So, having excluded fire and theft from the policy, I'm sure you're wondering what exactly IS covered. Well, third party of course. And accidental damage. With particular reference to wild animals. Which, living in a countryside over-run with wild boar, is particularly useful.

Monday 3rd
RIP Kenwood.

Yesterday was a sad day; our Kenwood BM200 bread machine gave up the ghost. I'd put all the ingredients in the bread pan, but when I plugged the machine in to the mains, it gave a last, sad, feeble chirrup and the display went blank. It wasn't the fault of the plug or the socket. So it looks like we'll need to get another bread maker. Still, I can't complain; it's been used on average twice a week. Every week. For twelve years.

As I hate getting my fingers sticky with dough, LSS finished kneading the dough mix by hand in a bowl, and then we baked it in our Panasonic Dimension 4 Genius combination microwave/grill/oven. This is starting to sound like an advertisement for kitchen gear! But I just wanted to point out that the oven has been used daily since I bought it. And it's just turned eighteen.

Thursday 6th

Last night the temperature dipped to minus four degrees Centigrade. The pond had frozen over, and it stayed that way for most of the day. We did our usual weekly shopping in Salbris, taking extra care on the road because this one in particular has a tendency to have patches of black ice in places.

The afternoon was spent cutting more wood with the chainsaw. The workshop is now nearly empty of scrap bits of wood; we had been using one end of the workshop to store all the old bits of timber we had come across whilst de-junking the house and outbuildings.

As far as garden produce goes, we're still eating watermelons, although now we only have one remaining! Not bad going - eating watermelons in December in the northern hemisphere!

Friday 7th

Last night we had the first snow of the season; we awoke to find everything covered with around 5cm of the white stuff. It snowed off and on during the day, and then turned to rain. This effectively melted all the snow and left slushy puddles everywhere.

All the bonsai trees excepting the big pine were moved indoors a couple of days ago; because the pots are very shallow the roots are susceptible to frost. The big one is in a deeper pot, so it can stay outside for a bit longer.

Sunday 9th

WE HAVE WATER! Yesterday I connected the final section of copper piping leading from the pressure vessel in the loft to the kitchen. This morning I turned on the main tap, and inspected my handiwork for leaks. There was one, where a soldered joint had not been fully sealed, so I re-soldered it. We now have clean borehole water all the way to the kitchen sink! The next tasks are the fabrication of a thermal store, and the installation of the boiler stove. We'll then have hot water too. What luxury!

Tuesday 18th

Today we had breakfast for lunch.

I shall explain.

The aged FIL has quite a bit of old farm equipment, not in very good condition, which neither he nor we will ever use. So he's agreed that we can try and sell it for him, and he'll give us a commission. There are ploughs, harrows, fertilizer spreaders, seeders, milk churns, cream separators – in fact, getting rid of all this stuff could take a while.

The French website we used to find our second-hand kitchen range has an agricultural section too. So LSS took some photographs of the first few items and listed them for sale online. Two weeks ago she received a phone call from Hungary, and the person expressed an interest in two of the ploughs. Despite promising to call back again, no such call took place.

Yesterday, LSS received another phone call from a person with a heavily-accented Eastern European accent.

"Oh no you don't!" she said. "I'm not reserving the ploughs for another Hungarian that never calls back."

"Not at all," the woman reassured her. "I'm not Hungarian. I'm Romanian. And I'm actually just an interpreter for a couple of blokes that buy old farm equipment in France. They deliver stuff to France, and instead of going back with an empty truck, they buy old farm stuff and sell it here at a profit."

Fair enough. LSS was concerned, however, regarding the larger of the two ploughs.

"This thing is heavy. Can the lorry cope with it?" she asked.

"Oh yes, that's not a problem. They're collecting two small tractors from another farm as well. The lorry is an articulated 25-tonner. By the way, do you have a forklift?"

<Insert red flashing warning light here...>

"No, I'm afraid not," LSS replied.

"Never mind, I'm sure they'll find a way to load the plough. I'll give you a call when they reach your village tomorrow morning."

So this morning we rose early, as we usually do, lit the wood stove; and put a saucepan of porridge on to cook. This did not even have time to reach simmering point when the phone rang. The Romanian lorry had arrived in the village and they wanted to know the way to the aged FIL's farm.

We dropped everything, took the porridge off the stove, and drove into the village to fetch them. The lorry was very easy to find as it was the only large vehicle in the village. It was, indeed, an articulated type. We led them to the aged FIL's farmhouse.

Now in case you didn't know, an articulated lorry consists of two parts; the front is called the "tractor unit" (not to be confused with a farm tractor), and the rear bit (which normally carries all the goods) is called a "semi-trailer".

There were two men in the cab. When they stopped the lorry and climbed down, we discovered that there was a small problem. Neither of them spoke French. Both of them spoke Romanian. Which I suppose is normal if you're Romanian. Neither LSS nor I speak Romanian.

Neither of them spoke English, and Dutch was a no-go as well. I didn't bother asking if they spoke Swahili, of which I know a few words. Now we need some names here; I can't go calling them "first chap" and "second chap". And due to the language barrier we never did find out their real names. So I shall call the first one Dmitri (for no other reason than that it sounds Romanian) and the second shall be known as Ivan (because I looked it up and Ivan is a Romanian name).

It transpired that Dmitri knew a bit of German, and as I had learned German at school, a three-way translation immediately took place. LSS explained which farm equipment was for sale, and how much it was, in English to me. I translated this into German (with many French words thrown in accidentally, because I hadn't spoken German for thirty years) to Dmitri, and Dmitri explained it in Romanian to Ivan. (Ivan was the one doing the buying, not Dmitri. Dmitri was the main driver. Ivan was also a driver, but did the buying.

187

I've said that already, but I just wanted you to be as confused as we were.)

So Ivan selected one of the ploughs. He then asked (through Dmitri) whether we had a forklift (were you paying attention earlier?)

Oh dear.

No, we replied.

Dmitri then explained in German that the plough was too heavy to be lifted onto the semi-trailer without one.

I said we knew that.

Ivan spotted the aged FIL's tractor in the barn and pointed it out to Dmitri. I forestalled the obvious next question by explaining that this tractor was too large to be able to drive into the semi-trailer carrying the plough (which would have to be put in sideways anyway), and the rear hydraulics could not lift the plough to a sufficient height to put it on the semi-trailer.

Ivan then said something to Dmitri, Dmitri repeated it to me in German, and I repeated it to LSS in English. It was along the lines of: "We have to fetch another two tractors this morning from a place about 100km away, and we'll return this afternoon. We'll hitch the plough to one of the small tractors, and drive it onto the lorry with ramps." Fine, we said.

At this stage I should also point out that Dmitri and Ivan had already collected two old tractors, which were right at the front of the semi-trailer.

This is when things started going wrong. Dmitri and Ivan jumped into the lorry, drove it forward around a ninety-degree left-hand bend in the road, and then started to reverse it into the farm courtyard. Now you may have heard some tales about Romanian truck drivers. Ice Road Truckers they ain't. The lorry immediately made its way into the deep ditch on the left of the road where it stuck. I fetched the tractor, but this proved to have insufficient power to extract the lorry from the ditch. Dmitri and Ivan then attempted to unhitch the semi-trailer from the tractor unit, without much success because of the angle of the cab relative to the entire rig. I remember thinking at the time this seemed to be an odd thing to do.

LSS went into the aged FIL's farmhouse and telephoned a neighbour who had a larger tractor. He was kind enough to drop everything and bring the four-wheel-drive monster over.

Unfortunately, even this beast did not have sufficient power. Not only that, but during the tug-of-war, oil started pouring out of the tractor transmission from a burst oil seal. We obviously needed a winch.

Fortunately the neighbour had a brother who was also a farmer not too far away. This brother had an even larger tractor with a winch. After another telephone call, a visit was arranged. It was now 11 a.m. The neighbour's brother (whom I will call NB for short) turned up at 2 p.m. Well, he had to have lunch first of course, which I suppose was fair enough. We took advantage of the lull in events to scoot off home and have lunch as well. In other words, we ate the porridge. The wood stove had of course died out by this time so we finished cooking the porridge on the gas stove.

We returned to the scene of the action just before 2 p.m. When NB arrived, he examined the situation, and ran out a length of steel winch cable to the front of the lorry, where it was attached to the chassis with a steel shackle. NB asked me to ask Dmitri if he was sure the semi-trailer was still properly attached to the tractor unit after their abortive efforts to unhitch it earlier.

"Yes," he replied.

Well, you will by now have realised that something else was waiting to happen. Of course the semi-trailer was not attached properly to the tractor unit. The powerful winch on the NB's tractor pulled the cab out of the ditch all right. However this was accompanied by a ripping, grinding noise as the tractor unit separated from the semi-trailer, tearing off most of the left-hand rear mudguard. The now unsupported semi-trailer twisted slowly to one side with a groaning noise, burying the front left support leg in the ditch, in the hole which had been created by the left rear wheel of the cab. The right-hand rear wheels of the semi-trailer were now in the air.

Dmitri leapt into action to repair the rear mudguard of the tractor unit, tying it on again with bits of wire, whilst NB re-positioned his tractor at the rear of the semi-trailer, where he attached the winch cable to one of the two tractors inside the trailer in order to redistribute some of the weight to the rear. The tractor was pulled towards the rear doors of the semi-trailer. (No, I know what you're thinking. It didn't fall out. Although that would probably have been a fitting Next Phase of The Saga). The other tractor was also moved towards the rear doors, this one under its own steam.

With the weight re-distributed, NB then attached a pulley to a large oak tree using a canvas strop. The winch cable was passed through this pulley and then attached to the side of the front chassis of the semi-trailer. In no time at all the front of the semi-trailer was extracted from the ditch and aligned on the roadway again.

Dmitri then reversed the tractor unit underneath the semi-trailer, joining the two together again. Whilst he was thus engaged, NB re-coiled his winch wire, and then went over to Dmitri and Ivan. Despite not speaking a word of Romanian, he made the two of them understand that this had taken up two hours of his time, which he would normally have employed more usefully elsewhere, and as a result the charge for the extraction would be €80. I had to hide a smile - bang went their profit for the day. Tucking the notes into his hip pocket, he then went inside the farmhouse to say hello to the aged FIL. I stayed to watch, just in case there were Further Developments.

There were. Dmitri was now unable to successfully reverse the semi-trailer around the right-angle corner. And before you say "Ah, but it was probably not possible to do so", I would point out that the aged FIL used to have earthmoving equipment. We're talking big Caterpillar-type machines here. On a low-loader. The sort which need to be accompanied on public roads by escort vehicles. The sort of low-loader which was articulated. Which he frequently turned around in the farmyard.

Their only option was – wait for it - to ask NB to reattach the winch to the side of the rear of the semi-trailer, and pull it sideways around the corner. (This was done free of charge actually! I had visions of NB asking them for another €40.)

By now NB had had enough, and pointed the winch-end of his tractor homewards. Dmitri and Ivan then (probably wisely) decided that the best way to get back to the main road was by reversing all the way there, a distance of about a kilometre. I fetched a shovel and busied myself filling in the monstrous holes left in the farm road by the extraction procedures.

We've decided we're not going to sell any other large farm equipment unless the buyer either fetches it with a tractor, or loads it themselves onto a smaller lorry. No articulated vehicles allowed.

Needless to say we didn't see Dmitri and Ivan again. I wonder if they know Boris and Igor?

Oh of course – you haven't met Boris and Igor. Well, if you're sitting comfortably, let me introduce you.

When I was working in IT in central London, the company had decided to replace all the leased Xerox multifunction copiers with Canons.

The leasing company was therefore asked to collect the first of these machines, and I was asked to show the removal men where it was. Now, bear in mind that this was a copier which was working perfectly, but the Canons had a bit more functionality. Also, this particular Xerox model had a decorative back panel which proudly displayed the brand name.

The removal men duly turned up. For the sake of this narrative I will call them Boris and Igor (they were Eastern European). They arrived in a large white van; I noticed at the time it did not have a tail lift; neither did they have any sort of trolley. I thought this was a bit odd as these machines are quite heavy. I took them up to the 7th floor to show them where the device was. Boris said something to Igor which presumably meant "you grab that end and I'll push from here". Igor grabbed the output stacker tray and lifted.

Snap.

"Oh dear," I thought. I told them to be more careful, and pointed out that they would need to remove the back panel in order to get it through the narrow doorway leading to the lift. Blank looks resulted. Boris pushed mightily from one end and the machine started to move. I leaped out of the way, switching the machine off at the wall and unplugging it in mid-leap. The machine reached the doorway.

Igor then said something to Boris, presumably "Um, this ain't going to go through 'ere." Boris turned to me and asked, "You haf screwdriving?" It turned out they had not brought any tools with them. I told them I did, and would go and fetch one. Igor came down in the lift with me. Leaving him in the Reception area, I went into the IT Department.

I located a screwdriver and returned to Reception. Igor was missing. I went up to the 7th floor. Boris was missing, too. I removed the decorative back panel and after waiting forlornly for a few minutes for the missing removal men, returned to the lobby. As I reached it, Igor came through the door, closely followed by Boris, proudly carrying a brand new set of screwdrivers from a hardware shop nearby. I didn't have the heart to follow them upstairs.

Now, the entrance to the building had two glass doors, on either side of a revolving glass centre door. This revolving centre door could be moved to one side in order to allow wide loads through. However, as luck would have it, I was called away from my current position as interested spectator in order to attend to a minor computer crisis elsewhere.

Ten minutes later I returned to the lobby. The receptionist was staring in horror at the scene. She had told them that the central door could be moved to one side; they had thanked her, and then forced the Xerox through the narrow left-hand doorway. I was very impressed; I had been certain that it would not have fitted through the gap. Observing the deep scratches on the front and back of the machine, I returned to the IT Department to make sure that everyone was in agreement that the 7th floor Xerox had been in perfect unblemished working order.

At this stage I should also point out that there are two long, fairly high steps leading from the pavement to the glass entry doors. Going back to the lobby, I saw that the way that Boris and Igor had chosen to solve this particular problem was to simply push the machine down the steps. (Once they had gone, like a good citizen, I picked up all the little bits of plastic from the pavement.)

Now this is where a truck tail lift would have been useful. Having trundled the now thoroughly wobbly machine across the pavement, they then realised that the back of the white van was higher than the kerb. I couldn't bear to watch, so I went for a short walk (Company Health & Safety rules dictated that I was not allowed to move equipment of this type). When I returned ten minutes later they had gone.

However, that's not the end of the tale. Two weeks later, the phone rang.

"Hello, Leasing Company Administration Department here. What was the last meter reading on the Xerox?"

"!"

During the conversation which followed, I explained that we did not have the latest reading on file, and the Xerox would need to be switched on in order to take the current meter reading.

The following day, the phone rang again.

"Hello, Leasing Company Administration Department here again. Just to let you know that the Xerox won't switch on. It's coming up with an error message. We've contacted Xerox, but they won't send an engineer out because the machine is not at the contractual registered address. But don't worry, we'll sort this out."

The day afterwards, I received a call from the receptionist. "There's a Xerox in reception which has just been delivered, do you know anything about it?"

Due to the lack of space, the only place to put the Xerox was ... you've guessed it ... back in the office on the 7th floor. A couple of beefy blokes from the administration department duly trundled the Xerox upstairs, where it was plugged in and switched on. Surprise, surprise, the screen displayed a "hardware failure" message.

Covered by the terms of the service contract, a Xerox engineer was requested to repair the machine. He turned up and proceeded to replace some broken bits. This took him two visits. At the end of the second day he reported to me that the Xerox was up and running again.

"Of course," he said, "I've had to replace several parts. One of these was the network controller board. So I'm afraid your meter readings have been reset to zero."

I waited expectantly for Boris and Igor to take the machine away again, but they never returned.

When I left the company two years later the Xerox had been moved to an empty office on the 2nd floor. And for all I know it could still be there.

January

THE barn roof is insulated, and construction of a thermal store begins. The motorcycle insurance saga continues.

Friday 4th

During these dark days of winter, I have been working on some more pages for the website. It's been too cold to do any outside jobs except for those which are essential.

As the weather prompted me to work indoors, I've been insulating the roof of the adjoining barn, because that's where the water supply pipes and pressure vessel reside. We would rather not have the pipes freeze when the temperature dips below zero. I've nearly finished this; the insulation involves cutting appropriately-sized pieces of glass fibre and stuffing these pieces in between the rafters. They are then held in position by strips of hardboard. The task is nearly complete. Of course when it is time to install the thermal solar panel on the roof, a section of this work will need to be undone.

Our festive fare consisted of primarily roast wild boar and an assortment of home-grown vegetables. We had the obligatory escargots in garlic butter, but made up for it by having a traditional English Christmas pudding. We bought this last year before leaving the UK. One thing I do like about France is the enormous number of varieties of cheese, so we also had a good selection of these. Well, I have to keep my strength up somehow...

Wednesday 9th

It would seem that the motorcycle insurance saga has not quite finished.

Yesterday I received a recorded letter, dated 31st December. It should have been collected last week, but the local post office was closed for a week, so I was only able to fetch it yesterday. It was from the insurance company, Generali Belgium.

Basically it says I have until the 11th January to provide the "Relevant Information".

I had no idea what relevant information they require, so once again LSS called the broker, Agence Eaton. It seemed that the problem lay with the proof of my previous no claims bonus, issued by my previous insurance company in the UK, Motorcycle Direct.

Shock, horror. It's in English. And Generali Belgium cannot read English, despite this being an official language of Europe; so they have decided that they are no longer going to insure me. This is three months after they received all the documentation, mind you.

However, the broker informed LSS that they had now found another insurance company, Generali Belgium, which will insure me. It's slightly more expensive, €460 this time. Although this time the insurance policy does include theft. With a hefty excess of €1500.

And no, I didn't make a mistake with the name of the company. Generali Belgium was what they said. The name of the previous company which has decided it doesn't want to insure me?

Generali Belgium.

No, I don't understand it either.

Thursday 10th

Agence Eaton called back this morning and have now come up with an explanation.

They originally went via an intermediary based in Paris called Solly Azar. Solly Azar deals with Generali Belgium because their prices are cheaper. However, Generali Belgium is fussier when it comes to documentation. Also, in France, insurance companies give themselves three months to decide whether or not they will actually insure you. (So be warned, if you have taken out a new French insurance policy you may not actually be covered!)

So the outcome is that Agence Eaton will handle the insurance policy themselves, and the actual insurance company involved will be Generali France (not Generali Belgium, as they had mistakenly said in their last communication) which works slightly differently. Because Agence Eaton will handle the insurance themselves instead of going through an intermediary, they keep all the paperwork; and were thus able to confirm that they are indeed happy with the English documentation.

The only down side is that Generali France is one-third more expensive than Generali Belgium; but as I mentioned, insurance against theft is once again included in the policy. This is because they do not require every part of the motorcycle to be French security-marked. The other good news is that the excess is between €400 and €800, and not €1500 as they mentioned yesterday.

Documentation will apparently be sent for signature later today. But we've heard that line before.

Saturday 12th

Today was another wood-cutting day. I had pruned some of the branches of the chestnut trees across the road, and these have now been converted into woodstove-sized logs. They were all dead branches, and as a result are fairly dry, so can be used straight away.

The barn roof insulation is now complete, and I have started the next challenge, building the thermal store. I have drilled the required holes in the 500-litre galvanized steel cylinder I will be using (this was kindly donated to us by our neighbours T&M). However, I need an oxy-acetylene torch to fix the brass pipe connectors to the tank. I've looked into the price of hiring or purchasing one of these, but it's way too expensive for just one job. Apparently LSS's cousin JP (of *ballon* repair fame) has an industrial-sized oxy-acetylene set, so we'll have to wait until he has a minute to bring it to us - or for a convenient moment for us to go and fetch it. I do have a mig welder, and access to the aged FIL's arc welder, and also a brazing torch, but none of these are suitable for the job!

The kitchen electrical upgrade has also taken another step forward; the lighting circuit is now complete which means we have two new light switches installed. This also means there are no more dangling electric wires in the kitchen!

I've also installed a new kitchen cupboard which we bought at BricoDepot about a month ago. The room is now starting to look more like a kitchen! The next task: installing the new stainless steel sink.

In my spare time I have repaired the original household water supply system which we now use for the garden hosepipe, or washing the car. (I'm referring to the *"ballon"* fed by the well). The system is now working as designed; we no longer have to go and manually switch on the pump when we want to use the hosepipe. The galvanized steel cylinder given to us by T&M had a three-phase electrical pressure switch attached, so I used this switch, replacing our faulty one which had been wired up by the aged FIL. I wired it up correctly this time. The pump itself is also three phase (380V). It would appear that the aged FIL was not, after all, a competent electrician. He had wired the original three-phase pressure switch to a single-phase supply. I'm surprised it actually worked at all when we plugged it in.

On a three-phase plug, there are four wires. These are usually colour-coded as follows:

A yellow/green wire (the earth), a blue wire (neutral), and two live wires, red and brown respectively.

This is how the aged FIL had wired the pump:

Earth wire: yellow/green.

Neutral wire: yellow/green.

Live phase 1: yellow/green.

Live phase 2: yellow/green.

Sunday 20th

It snowed fairly steadily last night, and for most of the day. The large pine bonsai is now also indoors for protection against the low temperatures. I am a bit concerned that it may now be too warm for them, but we don't really have anywhere else they can be kept. We definitely need a greenhouse or polytunnel.

Cat is not at all bothered about the snow. I don't think she's a cat at all. I think she's a disguised Labrador. She doesn't even mind getting wet.

It's a good thing that we don't need to go anywhere today. Except for visiting the aged FIL of course, because the carers who normally get him out of bed and feed him are unwilling to risk the perilous journey to the deepest darkest countryside. So LSS has taken over the job for today. Although the main roads between the larger towns are cleared of snow by salting, the minor ones are untouched. And unlike in the mountainous areas of France, here it is not a legal requirement to fit winter tyres to your car. It doesn't snow frequently enough for that.

February

EATING food well past its use-by date, and I make some marmalade.

Thursday 7th

We've just finished dinner - a courgette and ham quiche with green beans, followed by a pudding of tinned pineapple slices. "So what?" you may ask. Well, let me give you some background to today's meal.

The late MIL was a little girl during the Second World War. France at that time was, of course, occupied; and as her family were tenant farmers, they received a lot of unwanted attention from the Wehrmacht, who confiscated the majority of the food. MIL was the youngest of ten children, and I think this scarcity of food affected her psychologically. She had the tendency to hide food in the oddest of places. Open a cupboard full of clothes, and there, lurking underneath a moth-eaten shirt, would be a packet of biscuits. Packets of sweets would peek out from behind the best china cups, and hidden in the rabbit shed you would find a tin of strawberry jam or a bottle of wine.

After the late MIL passed away a couple of years ago, LSS attempted a major clearout of rubbish, and many food items came to light. Unfortunately most of the dry goods like packets of biscuits, rice, or pasta, were either mouldy, or just stale and inedible. Nothing was wasted though; the carp were very well-fed.

Well, not everything was discovered. Last week LSS found an additional two items which had been exceptionally well-hidden, and we have just finished eating them this evening - to wit, a Kilner jar of green beans harvested soon after Chernobyl (bottled September 1987); and a tin of Kenyan pineapple slices - "consume before December 1988". Well, the tin *was* a bit rusty. But only on the outside. The pineapples tasted fine! And the green beans tasted - well, like green beans normally taste. A bit tingly on the tongue though.

Bless her cotton socks!

Sunday 17th

We've been in the habit of buying mandarin oranges over the past few weeks, especially as it has transpired the aged FIL likes them. So these have become an additional source of nutrition and Vitamin C for this particularly fussy eater.

Unfortunately the last batch we bought from Carrefour was actually pretty inedible. They were incredibly difficult to peel, and exceedingly bitter. So I decided to make some marmalade. What an improvement! I may have to make some more...

March

N ow that the weather has improved, work on the thermal store continues, and I construct a wood stove from an old electric water heater. Some vehicle maintenance takes place, and we look back at the past year.

Saturday 9th
Work on various projects has been progressing slowly. The thermal store has now been moved to the loft, and placed above a supporting wall. Because it will contain five hundred litres of water, it would be a bad idea to have the half-ton weight supported by only a couple of ceiling joists. The boiler stove has also been placed in its final position, and I've started joining the sections of 22mm diameter copper pipe to connect it to the thermal store. Holes have already been drilled in the ceiling.

As the weather was fairly good today, I finally completed the roof of the wood shed, using several panels of corrugated iron. The wood shed itself was constructed out of recycled wooden pallets. It's now ready to be filled with firewood for next winter. A couple of large branches from last year's fallen oak tree have already been cut into woodstove-sized lengths and split into firewood.

I also took the opportunity to get rid of all the rubbish in the brazier, and make some more charcoal at the same time.

My collection of bonsai trees, which have been inside the house for the winter, are now once again outdoors, and have also been re-potted. All but two are not looking too happy though; it may have been a bit too warm for them indoors.

I recently recovered an old 100-litre electric water cylinder from the aged FIL's barn, and have been dismantling it with a view to turning it into a wood stove to heat my workshop, which is absolutely freezing in the winter (obviously). Much welding and grinding has been taking place; and the end result could well look like a piece of steampunk art. I haven't used any bits of polished brass, though, so it probably doesn't qualify.

I've also serviced LSS's Hyundai which has just reached 60,000 miles. I installed a K&N air filter and some Denso Iridium spark plugs, so this means these items will not need to be replaced again for the foreseeable future. My Honda ST1100 (I did receive the insurance document) is currently without wheels, as I've just had new tyres fitted and am taking the opportunity to replace the clutch and brake hoses with stainless steel ones, as well as installing new stainless steel pistons in the brake callipers. Once it's all back together again I may be able to go for a ride - presuming the weather stays fine and the road is passable.

Speaking of the road, we had a visit this week from the *Garde Champêtre*, who was inspecting the state of the public road which runs past the property. It seems the road is going to be repaired shortly (and it's high time it was; it's a mud bath).

Sunday 24th

Day 365 since the shipwreck. The daily ritual of scanning the horizon for a passing ship had the same result; emptiness was again the norm. Sighing, I wandered back up the beach to my crude bamboo shelter, and passed the time by sorting my fish scale collection; this time according to size and colour.

Oops, wrong scene... I think the French countryside is getting to me.

It's hard to believe we've been here a year today. I looked again at my "To Do" list, feeling certain that we hadn't achieved very much over the past year. But it's been reassuring to see that there are a lot of entries with lines scratched through them. Here are just a few:

- Make house less damp by installing gutters - check.

- Install a rainwater recovery system for watering the garden in summer - check.

- Build a wood shed to store all our firewood - check.

- Have a borehole installed - check.

- Install a cold water supply to the house to replace the rusty water from the well - check.

- Build a thermal store - check.

- Install new double-glazed doors and windows to help with keeping the house warm in winter - check.

- Upgrade the outdated electricity wiring - well, the kitchen is done. And the lounge. I haven't started on the bedroom yet, but at least all the antique fuses have been replaced with proper circuit breakers and a proper earth system with lightning protection has been installed. So I think that qualifies as a check.

- Cure the problem we were experiencing with mould - check. Well, so far, so good.

- Stop the pond from encroaching into the garden by repairing the erosion at the edges - nearly complete. Unfortunately with all the rain we've had, the pond is now full, so I will need to wait until the water level drops a bit before this job can be finalized. I did however manage to dig a trench from the pond to the closest drainage ditch so that an overflow pipe could be installed.

- Start a website about the project - check.

Of course, like all lists, ours just keeps growing, no matter how many items are crossed out! So it looks like Year Two will be just as busy.

So how have we done on the budget front? Year one has seen us spend 40% of our total budget. Our largest expenditures thus far have been the rainwater recovery system and the double-glazed doors and windows. Everything else is well under budget; and this even includes our living expenses. Of course the garden is helping tremendously in this respect.

I think the following year should be a great deal easier as we now know our way around at least some parts of the French system. At least we don't have any further vehicle registrations to do. No more *Quittus Fiscals* here, thank you very much!

About the Author

Robert Martin was born in Uganda in 1963. He graduated with a BSc degree in Forestry and Nature Conservation in 1987. He has also been in Kenya, Tanzania, Australia, South Africa, Namibia and the United Kingdom.

He now resides in France with his wife Caroline, where he is currently renovating a nineteenth century farmhouse, and attempting to learn the French words for sundry building materials.

Author of the money-saving guide "How To Survive a Recession", he is also the creator and administrator of several websites:

http://www.st-1100.com
http://www.landyrebuild.com
http://www.stampswops.com
http://www.la-darnoire.com

www.ingramcontent.com/pod-product-compliance
Lightning Source LLC
Chambersburg PA
CBHW060237050426
42448CB00009B/1477